YOU'RE TELLING ME!

YOU'RE TELLING ME!

WHY WE ARE SO GOOD AT
COMMUNICATING WITH EACH OTHER

BY NANCY APPLEYARD

Matador
9 Priory Business Park,
Wistow Road, Kibworth Beauchamp,
Leicestershire. LE8 0RX
Tel: 0116 279 2299
Email: books@troubador.co.uk
Web: www.troubador.co.uk/matador
Twitter: @matadorbooks

ISBN 978 1838594 459

British Library Cataloguing in Publication Data.
A catalogue record for this book is available from the British Library.

Printed and bound in the UK by TJ International, Padstow, Cornwall
Typeset in 13pt Gill Sans by Troubador Publishing Ltd, Leicester, UK

Matador is an imprint of Troubador Publishing Ltd

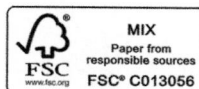

Thank you Keith
Thank you Jools

OTHER BOOKS BY NANCY APPLEYARD

The Minimum Core for Language and Literacy
Communicating with Learners in the Lifelong Learning Sector
The Professional Teacher in Further Education
Reflective Teaching and Learning in Further Education
Lesson Planning: Getting It Right in a Week

CONTENTS

INTRODUCTION   VIII

BODY LANGUAGE
   1. Every Body Does: what our body might say about us   3
   2. Face Facts: what our face might say about us   15
   3. More Than Words: why speaking needs a little help   27
   4. Figuratively Speaking: why our bodies speak   38

LANGUAGE
   5. It's English – Innit: how we get language to work for us   52
   6. Breaking The Code: how we make sense of English   66
   7. The Chattering Species: how we first learned to speak   80
   8. A Mini History: how we changed language   92

COMMUNICATING
   9. Getting The Message Across: what happens when we talk to each other   109
  10. Getting The Meaning: why talking can be tricky   121
  11. Diversity in Action: how we are the same but different   132
  12. Every Body Feels: how body language may have helped us to survive   144

AFTERWORD   156

INTRODUCTION

We are unique. We are the only inhabitants of this earth that uses spoken language, our voice and our body in seamless harmony to interact with others. The rewards for our dedication to this engaging activity have been monumental. Indeed, our unrivalled ability to communicate, co-operate and collaborate may have helped to ensure our survival and to enable us to flourish. The story of what we have achieved is remarkable. It is the story first told by Charles Darwin, of the survival of our individual selves and the incredible success of our species. It is a story of how and why we communicate with each other and of why we are so skilled at what we do. It is also a celebration of our phenomenal expertise.

The story is told in the three parts of this book. The theme of part one is body language. If using our bodies to communicate with each other has helped to ensure our survival what is it that our bodies are able to do? In this first part you will discover how our bodies talk to each other through our facial expressions, our gestures and the sound of our voices and you will learn how and why we might have first learned to use our bodies in this way.

Language is the theme of the second part of the book. If language has brought us immense success, what is our relationship with it? This second part offers a light-hearted look at the nature the English language, delves into the way we interact with it and manipulate it for our own purposes and then explores how and why we might have first learned to speak and then to develop language.

The third part of the book describes what happens every time we interact with another person. If our capacity to communicate is showcased through our expertise, how is this played out in our everyday interactions? This final part highlights our unique approach to communicating and provides some possible answers for why we are so skilled at language and why our bodies are so adept at conveying information about us to others.

As you read through each of the chapters you will find a number of opportunities to try out a variety of activities. These appear under the heading TRY THIS. Some of these activities are questions, mostly just for you to think about; others are more direct, asking you for an answer. Yet others involve a small task and a couple of them will suggest you do them with another person. Each of the activities is designed to give you a particular experience and some will illustrate a preceding statement. Just go for the ones that appeal to you.

One final note: it concerns the word 'communication'. There's little doubt that this word has a bad press. Mention it at any gathering and the immediate response is a glazing over of the eyes and a rapid change of subject. Its shoddy reputation is very much undeserved. How we communicate with each other, something we all do throughout our lives, provides us with a window through which we are able to gently and good naturedly observe ourselves.

BODY LANGUAGE

You might not realise it but you are an expert at body language. Think for a moment about what happens when you pass someone on a narrow pavement. You advance towards each other and nine times out of ten you know who will pass on the left and who on the right. You don't need to think about it, you just know what their next action is going to be. You could say that your two bodies are in conversation with each other. The word expert doesn't really do justice to this phenomenal skill that each of us possesses.

Yet there is much more to body language than negotiating your way past another person on a narrow pavement. Consider that time of year when the GCSE and A level results come out. If you watch the news on the TV you certainly won't have failed to notice the body language of the students as they receive their grades. Acute signs of jubilation or dejection are the order of the day. On the one hand you will see broad grins, arms raised high and possibly jumping up and down: on the other hand, you might see mouths turned down, hunched shoulders and bowed bodies. It would be impossible to misinterpret what is going on here.

Just like these lucky or not so lucky students, what we might be thinking and feeling on a day-to-day, minute-to-minute basis is available to all who might care to take an interest in observing us. It will be available to them through our bodies in numerous different ways. It will be there in our gestures and in the way we position and move our body; this is the topic of chapter one. You will see it in the expression on our face; the topic of chapter two. You will hear it in the sound of our voice: this is the major theme of chapter three. How and why we might have first learned to communicate with each other through our bodies is the theme of chapter four.

1

EVERY BODY DOES:
WHAT OUR BODY MIGHT SAY ABOUT US

Did you glance at the picture below before reading these words? My guess is that you did. We are drawn to images. Pick up a newspaper or magazine and your eyes will immediately make their way to anything visual. Only after you have checked out the pictures will you begin to read through the text. The explanation for our love of pictures is that they are easy for us, we can 'get the picture' instantly and work out what is happening with little effort on our part. This is how we check out other people and we do it whilst on autopilot. Bodies are visual, 3D images that are easy for anyone to see, instantly. What's more, they are animated, moving images; what could be better?

We have a beautiful and sumptuous spoken and written language. Yet when it comes to interacting with others, words alone are not sufficient for our complex human communicative needs. Luckily, words are not left to do this vital job unaided. Our bodies are in the same business, communicating vigorously in numerous different ways and orchestrating a huge repertoire of gestures. Indeed it is well nigh impossible for us to interact with each other without using our body. We absolutely need to recruit our body whenever we are engaged in a face to face interaction with another person and we will use any part of it to do the job. We might raise our shoulders to shrug indifference, tap our feet if we are feeling impatient, nod our head when we are in agreement and so on. We use our heads, our hands and our arms freely and continuously. We use the way we position and move our bodies and we even use the way we present our body to the world.

Taken together, these different gestures play a huge role in all our interactions. In this chapter we take a look at some of these gestures in action to see what we might discover when we watch other people and what they might find out from watching us.

A SHOW OF HANDS

When you think about body language you might think of people you know who wave their arms around when they speak. It is true that just about every one of us will use our hands and arms to express ourselves, although many of us are unaware that we do so and some of us are certainly more expressive than others. When we are speaking our hands work a little like punctuation marks; they help us to regulate the timing and the rhythm of our spoken words. There is also something to be gained for our listeners when we use our hands when we speak. Our hand movements help them to understand and remember what they have heard us say. (To find out more Google: Beattie G & McLoughlin N, Pease & Pease.)

We can never say for sure that a particular gesture has a particular meaning and this applies across the board with body language. Each individual gesture needs to be seen in the same way as an individual word that might have several meanings. For example the word 'fine' can mean very good, sharp, delicate, subtle, or a sum of money paid to settle a matter. You are only able to understand the meaning once the word is inserted into a sentence.

4

Take for example the crossed arms gesture. What might it mean if you were talking to someone and they crossed their arms? There are many possibilities. It could indicate that they didn't much like or agree with what you were saying or indeed, that they didn't much like you. It could mean that they didn't understand what you were saying. It could mean that they were thinking hard about your words. Alternatively, it could mean that they were bored, or cold, or that they were just sitting comfortably, or something else. You would only be able to work out the meaning by looking at their other body signals. For example if they were smiling rather than scowling you could feel reasonably confident that they were more likely to be feeling comfortable rather than bored or puzzled.

TRY THIS

Stop reading for a moment and cross your arms. Keep them crossed for about ten seconds and then uncross them.

Now cross your arms again but this time cross them the other way round. If your right forearm was in front the previous time make sure your left arm is in front this time.

Was it as easy to cross your arms the other way round? Probably not: and were you surprised at the difference? One way certainly feels more comfortable possibly because we are more used to it. Yet the way we cross our arms may well have a genetic element as around seventy percent of us cross our left arm over our right arm. We don't really know why although it doesn't appear to be related to whether we are left or right handed.

We use our hands to make many of our greetings; the formal handshake and the friendly wave to someone we know. The origin of these gestures lies in allowing others see that we are a friend rather than a threat or a foe. When we hold our hands out in front of us to wave or shake hands for example, we are showing that we have no weapons hidden either close to our body or in our hands. Swearing an oath with our arm up and palm open means pretty much the same thing; that we are upright and trustworthy. Open hands are generally a sign of honesty and openness. Most of us find it difficult to tell a lie with our open palms exposed; this is because there is a close link between our gestures and our emotions.

If there is someone near you as you are reading this ask them to shake hands with you. Stop in mid-handshake and take note of the position of your two hands.

Are both hands positioned vertically to each other during the hand shake, in other words neither hand leaning forward or backward? Or is one of the hands leaning slightly forward so that some of the back of the hand is visible with the palm facing slightly down? This would inevitably mean that the other hand would be leaning slightly backward with the palm slightly up. If this is the case note which of you has the hand leaning forward with the palm down.

So what does this mean? It seems that the more dominant amongst us, those of us who feel more comfortable being in charge, are likely to turn their palms down when they shake hands so that some of the back of the hand is visible. Sometimes you see this when you observe politicians and world leaders shaking hands.

Most gestures where the palms face down tend to be dominant or power gestures. They include:

» downward movements with an open flat hand as if you are pushing someone down or patting a small child on the head,
» finger gestures with the finger pointing either outwards or downwards as in a jabbing motion,
» fist gestures and slicing or chopping gestures.

When we use palms down gestures we are metaphorically restraining our listeners, pushing them into obedience and attempting to force them to agree with us. Public speakers, especially politicians, will sometimes use them to vigorously promote or defend their ideas. Palms down gestures are often seen and felt as aggressive.

Palms up gestures usually mean the opposite. These are done with hands flat or lightly cupped and held out in front. Sometimes the arms are held out to the side as if you are about to embrace someone. With palms up gestures you are metaphorically begging for alms, requesting agreement. Again, politicians will sometimes use them when speaking to an audience and seeking their endorsement. Palms up gestures are usually seen as friendly and are mostly welcomed.

Hands also come in useful for offering a touch to others. Have you ever had the experience of giving a friendly touch on someone's arm and sensing that it makes them feel a little uncomfortable, or perhaps you have been on the receiving end of someone's touch and felt uncomfortable yourself? Some of us feel comfortable touching other people and will do it naturally and unconsciously while for others, a touch from another is a touch too personal.

On the whole, we feel more comfortable touching and being touched by people we are close to and less comfortable with those we know less well. Yet touch can be intended and interpreted as either positive or negative. It's also an interesting paradox. This paradox is illustrated in research which appears to show that if someone touches us, even if we don't know them, or are even aware that they have touched us, it may benefit us in some way. In this research a group of waiters were instructed to touch their customers when they took their orders. A control group was told not to touch their customers when taking their orders. The waiters who touched their customers received bigger tips than the non-touching waiters. (To find out more Google: Crusco & Wetzel 'The Midas Touch'.)

As you saw earlier with the handshake, touch can be used as a power gesture to indicate that you are in charge. Placing a hand on someone's upper arm or shoulder is another example. Although it's often a gesture of friendship it can also be used to dominate another person if the intention is to patronise them, a little like a pat on the head. You sometimes see politicians do this when they greet each other at meetings as they vie with each other for that alpha position. Sometimes this gesture accompanies a handshake. The politician's right hand reaches out to take the other person's hand; at the same time their left hand reaches out to hold or sometimes pat the other person's right arm or shoulder.

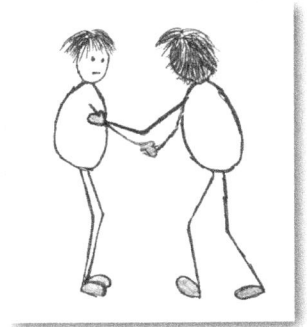

For the majority of us touch is most often experienced as a positive gesture. A gentle touch on the shoulder can indicate a friendly greeting or a gesture of support. A pat on the back often means congratulations. This gesture was used to congratulate actors in medieval theatre when the stage was positioned in the centre of the theatre. When the actors finished their performance they would need to exit the theatre through the audience and would receive congratulatory pats on the back as they passed. In modern theatres the stage is positioned at one end so the actors exit from the back of the theatre. Audiences have replaced the pat on the back with clapping.

Our hands can provide us with a useful way of swearing. Phallic gestures, such as the arm jerk and middle finger salute, so beloved of a small minority of football are far older than the game players of football. For example, the Roman historian Tacitus, when writing in the first century about the advance of the German tribesmen towards the Roman soldiers, takes note of the tribesmen's use of a middle finger salute.

Another swearing gesture is the two-finger salute. Its origins have been accredited to the story of the Battle of Agincourt, fiercely fought during the Hundred Year's War. The story goes that before the battle commenced the French troops mocked the English longbowmen, assuring them that their bow fingers would immediately be removed once the French had won the battle. When the English were victorious the longbowmen held up their two fingers to the French to mock them. This is a first-rate story but in fact it seems that the English longbow at the time may well have needed three fingers rather than two.

TALKING HEADS

Our heads are pretty versatile in conveying meaning. Take the head nod for example. Most of us will nod our head slightly to indicate that we are being attentive when listening to a speaker. Interestingly, a slow head nod can have a different meaning to a rapid head nod. Slow nodding can indicate that you are interested in what is being said whilst rapid nodding can mean the opposite. If you find yourself bored by what you are hearing nod your head quickly and it could well bring the speaker to a halt.

Nodding our head up and down means yes pretty much wherever you happen to be in the world. We can also nod our head to perform a short-cut version of the bow, a mini lowering of the body as a sign of deference, a gesture that has its roots in appeasement. So if nodding nearly always mean yes, does shaking your head from side to side always mean no? The answer is probably, at least as far as we know. It's thought to be the first gesture we learn. When being fed, newborn babies will turn their head to the side to indicate that they have had enough. Even chimpanzees have been observed shaking their heads to indicate refusal.

What does it mean if you lift your chin up and tilt your head back so that it gives the impression of looking down your nose. This gesture is more than likely to be interpreted as arrogance, a dominant gesture that gives an appearance of increased height. On the other hand tilting your head to one side by bringing your ear down towards your shoulder is likely to indicate the opposite. This is because this gesture exposes the jugular vein on the opposite side of your neck. It can be understood as a gesture of deference, one that is used by a number of other species to indicate surrender or appeasement.

BODY CHECK

Considering the body as a whole, how we sit, stand and move can provide us with a wealth of information. You need only to take a seat at the window in a café and watch the people passing by outside: as you enjoy your cappuccino you will get to view a whole range of body postures and movements. What can you learn from observing them? You know that you will see determined walkers, hurrying along with their head forward, their minds focused squarely on the task in hand. You are likely to see slow, hesitant walkers, preoccupied with other things and walkers who appear sad or worried, looking at the ground as if searching for a 5p piece they lost earlier. Yet other walkers will have their heads in the clouds dreaming of their next holiday.

Some of us are fortunate in having good body awareness, yet very few of us bother to take notice of what our bodies are doing. It's pretty much habit and habits are mostly unconscious. This isn't good news because if we habitually stoop or walk with our head down others will notice whilst we remain blissfully unaware.

How we feel will, to some extent, dictate what we do with our bodies. For example when we are feeling positive and cheerful we are likely to keep our head up and to look out at the world and when we are feeling a little sad our head will lower and our shoulders will droop. Yet this isn't the complete story. An example to illustrate arises when you think about the amount of space we might choose to occupy and the reasons for doing so. When we feel good we tend to take up more space and when we don't feel so good we take up less space. You only need to look at athletes at the end of a race to see this in action. The winners will throw their arms out and above their heads in triumph whilst the losers will stoop low with disappointment or even sink to the ground.

Yet there is more to this than meets the eye: indeed much more. It seems that this relationship between our feelings and the space we occupy is just as true in reverse.

Try this

Sit in a chair with your body in the following position for two minutes and note how you feel at the end. Put your feet flat on the floor, lean your upper body forward, hunch your shoulders, cross your arms in front of you and look down at your lap. In this position you are taking up little space.

Once the two minutes is up change to the following position, hold it for two minutes and note how you feel at the end. Lean your upper body back against the chair, spread your legs out in front of you (together or apart), stretch your arms out to the sides, perhaps leaning them on adjacent chair backs and look up and ahead. In this position you are taking up lots of space.

Which position did your prefer? It's likely to be the second with your body spread out. When we take up space it gives us a boost, makes us feel good; the more space our bodies take up the better and more positive we feel. On the other hand, the less space we take up the lower our spirits. Taking up space when sitting or standing is especially useful when we find ourselves in situations that can make us feel anxious, for example when waiting to be called in for an interview or to face the dentist's drill. The good feelings we get will give us the confidence to deal with what lies ahead. The temptation of course, when we feel anxious, is to do the opposite.

There are sound physiological reasons to explain why our feelings are so affected by our body position, reasons connected to the level of two hormones floating around in our blood. In essence, increasing the space we occupy increases the levels of testosterone. This is the hormone that can give us energy and good feelings. At the same time it decreases the levels of cortisol, the stress hormone. Stooping or sitting huddled up has the opposite effect. (To find out more Google: Cuddy A, TED talk.)

How much space we choose to take up is a strong indicator of confidence. Taller and bigger generally indicates confidence and even power and dominance. We can make ourselves appear more confident and powerful and better able to command others by standing tall, with head up. You can prove to yourself that size matters. Try telling someone off or giving them a command when you are sitting on a low seat and they are standing. It just doesn't work as well.

Lowering our body on the other hand, is usually seen by other people as non-threatening, a sign of deference. Its origins lie in appeasement and submission. A number of animal species, including dogs, will lower their body to appease a more dominant animal. We have formalised this lowering gesture into the bow and its variations, the head nod and the salutation where the hands are placed together as if in prayer and the head is lowered.

We can convey an immense amount of information about ourselves, not only by the way we stand, sit and move but also by the way we place ourselves in relation to others. For example getting too close to someone can pass an unwanted message and firmly put the brakes on a new relationship. Take the following scenario. You are at a meeting or a party; you find yourself with someone new and are chatting happily. Then you become aware that they are standing just a little too close for comfort and you feel crowded. You take a step back. They follow. Now you feel cornered. You have lost interest in them and what they are saying. You just want to escape. We can feel even more crowded and even threatened if the relationship between the other person and ourselves isn't equal. Say, for example, you are being questioned by a police officer or another authority figure; in this case you'll certainly want a little more space between the two of you.

Even where we choose to position ourselves in relation to someone else tells them something about us, perhaps how friendly we are and it can even reveal what our intentions might be.

TRY THIS

> You are attending a job interview or going for some professional advice. You enter the interview/consulting room. There is one interviewer/advisor. They come and greet you and offer you a seat at one end of a long rectangular table. They go and sit:
>
> At the other (far) end of the long table
> or
> At your end of the table, near to you and at right angles to you.
>
> What have you discovered about them from where they have chosen to place themselves in relation to you?

You will likely have made some personal judgements about them and their intentions based on where they have chosen to sit. Your assumptions about them may not necessarily be accurate but nevertheless, as far as you are concerned, you've learned that the interviewer/advisor who sat at the far end of the table prefers a more formal approach, may not be too friendly and might possibly be the boss, whilst the interviewer/advisor who sat nearer to you and at right angles is more casual, approachable and friendly.

ON STAGE

As you sit in that café with your cappuccino watching the world go by you may well be taking note of how those passers-by have chosen to present themselves to those around them. How we choose to bedeck and adorn our body is, for most of us, a pivotal feature of our personality. We have a powerful need, an aspect of our very humanness, to express ourselves though our body. Yet in doing so we give away a great deal of information about ourselves.

Sometimes we have no say about how we appear. Wearing a uniform is an example; others have made this decision for us. A uniform rule is a spoken or written rule of appearance. Yet it is the unspoken and unwritten rules about how we should appear that probably have a far greater influence on us, the rules of context and expectation. We need to be sure that we are not going to feel out of place or be embarrassed by the way we appear. How often have you asked yourself, 'Is this the right outfit for the 'do' I'm going to/meeting I have to attend?' Most of us find it difficult to step outside the expectations of what is appropriate for us and we are taken by surprise when this happens, if for example, we were introduced to an elderly person sporting neck tattoos and a nose ring.

Yet, at a deeper, more unconscious, level we are constantly displaying facets of our character, personality and inclinations, facets that are clearly available to others, through our choice of body adornment. The degree of formality we are comfortable with, our choice of colour, our use of body art, hair style and colour, make up, tattoos, jewellery and so on are examples. From these simple cues others observing us can gain insights into our occupation, our interests, our financial position and even our character and personality.

Notwithstanding this wealth of personal information we unconsciously make available to others, we can also use our appearance to make conscious, deliberate, specific statements about who we are; choosing to wear designer trainers or jeans for example. Our deliberate choices of adornment may be related to our particular group or tribe. Take the wearing of jewellery, an adornment with a long history of delineating group membership. To mark their affiliation to their tribe the Nuer women of South Sudan wear large, brightly coloured necklaces and headdresses, as do the women (and men) of the, now international Steam Punk tribe.

When it comes to image and adornment we are indeed fortunate because the ball is very much in our court. We can alter our appearance to suit whatever the context and our particular inclinations happen to be. We have the choice to present ourselves to the world in any way we choose.

» Just about everyone uses their hands when they speak; many of our greetings gestures indicate that we are friend not foe. Palms up gestures tend to be friendly whilst palms down gestures can indicate the opposite.

» Touch can be both positive and negative depending on the context. It is also a paradox as even though we are less comfortable being touched by those we don't know too well, a touch from a stranger may well benefit us.

» Head nodding and head shaking are generally considered to be universal gestures. Head shaking is thought to be innate and is shared by other primates. The head tilt to the side can indicate deference; the chin raised can indicate arrogance.

» Taking up space increases good feelings and levels of confidence: reducing space has the opposite effect.

» Most of us abide by the unspoken or unwritten rules that govern how we present ourselves; we use our appearance to make statements about ourselves and about our intentions.

Our bodies are immensely versatile in their ability to communicate with those around us; much of this dialogue is beneath our conscious radar. We are able to greet each other in a variety of ways, to dominate, to change the way others see us and to swear at each other without opening our mouths. Notwithstanding this superabundance of talent, our bodies do not operate in isolation but in harmony with the myriad expressions that our faces are able to display. This is the theme of the next chapter.

2

FACE FACTS:
WHAT OUR FACE MIGHT SAY ABOUT US

Have a look at the house below. Does it look a little like a face to you? If it does you are far from alone. Seeing faces in clouds or buildings or even everyday objects is so common it even has a name: pareidolia. Our eagerness to create faces compels many of us to compile them from a diversity of disparate lines and squiggles. There is even a distinct area in our brain that responds more strongly to images of faces than to images of anything else, specific brain cells that are devoted to processing faces. (To find out more Google: Tsao D, 'How the Brain Reads Faces', Scientific American.)

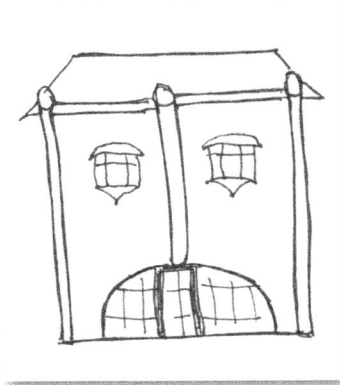

Our enthusiasm for faces begins the moment we are born. Tiny babies prefer to look at a face more than anything else; they seek them out from the fuzzy world that surrounds their not quite fully developed vision. It's as if they already know that a face means that food and comfort will be coming their way.

One possible reason to explain why faces are so important to us may lie in our distant past. In a tough world we would have needed to weigh up other people very quickly, to identify immediately whether someone was a friend who could provide help and support, or an enemy who might cause us harm. And we do appear to be hard wired to instantly recognise and respond to what we see when we look into the face of another human. This chapter will explore what another human's face might tell us about them and, of course, what our face is likely to be announcing to those around us. It will delve into some of our motivations, intentions and emotions as they are displayed on our face.

FACE VALUE

Unless we are one of a pair of identical twins we will have our own unique combination of facial features. We might occasionally think that we would perhaps prefer a face that is a little narrower or rounder, or we would like to have bigger eyes or a smaller nose. Hopefully we are more than happy with the face we have been allocated but our faces have significance beyond just aesthetics: they have a role to play in the way others judge us. It seems that within a second or two of meeting someone new, just by observing their face, we will have made judgements about them. For example, we might judge them to be aggressive, dominant, honest, outgoing, intelligent and so on simply from what we read in their expression. Interestingly most of us tend to make pretty similar judgements.

There are even occasions when the shape of our face and how our features are displayed on it could be to our advantage. Say, for example, you have what is sometimes called a 'baby face'. This is a rounded face, with large eyes, a large forehead and a smaller chin. If so, you are likely to get away with more than the rest of us because you are more likely to be judged as honest and trustworthy. (To find out more Google: Sporer S & Goodman J, 'Disparity in Sentencing Decisions'.)

The fact that every single person in the world has a unique face is quite staggering but additionally, our faces are supremely versatile in creating a plethora of expressions. Numerous facial muscles work in unison to allow us to create and convey around 250,000 expressions that can be recognised and understood by others. We are the only species on earth that has this repertoire of expression. (To find out more Google Birdwhistell R, 'The Language of the Body'.)

THE EYES HAVE IT

It's not difficult to see why our eyes have sometimes been called the windows to our soul; they can give away to the observer a goodly amount of information about us. Consider the pupils in our eyes; they will dilate when we are aroused, for example if we feel attraction, excitement or interest in someone or something, or if we detect a potential threat or identify an opportunity. Larger pupils allow an increase in the amount of light that enters our eyes so that we can see clearly what is in front of us. Larger pupils are usually seen as more attractive and there is a good reason why this is the case. Babies and young children have larger pupils than adults. This helps to ensure that adults are attracted to nurturing them. Eyes also have a vital role to play when we smile. When our smile is genuine our eyes will quite naturally crease and laughter lines form at outer edges. This doesn't happen when our smile isn't genuine; then we might say that the smile hasn't reached the eyes.

We are pretty skilled at making eye contact at a considerable distance; 30 or 40 metres would prove little problem for most of us and we can also tell, even at this distance whether someone has made eye contact with us.

When we are in conversation we use eye contact to synchronise our participation. Eye contact isn't exactly looking directly into someone's eyes and it's not staring at them. It is more of an ongoing, fairly frequent returning of our eyes to the other person's face, not directly to their eyes but close to them. We do this when we are speaking and also when we are listening. On the whole we make eye contact more often when we are listening and this is one way we let the speaker know that we are interested in what they are saying. Eye contact works a little like a good lubricator; it helps to ensure that the flow of the conversation is smooth.

Our eyebrows are worthy of a special mention. Although on a practical level they help to keep dirt and moisture away from our eyes, they also have an important role to play that may be closely linked to our past. Whilst other human species such as the Neanderthals had a pronounced bone ridge over their eyes, we don't: this lack of a bone ridge allows us to raise our eyebrows at will.

This ability to raise our eyebrows first occurred at a time when important social changes began to take place and humans first began exchanging gifts across large regions. It seems that our ancient ancestors raised their eyebrows to signal that they were not a threat to others that they might encounter. In other words when peoples from different tribes and kinship groups met it became possible to indicate friendly intentions. This ability would have helped to forge friendships across groups.

We modern humans use our eyebrows in the same way that our distant ancestors used them. When we see someone at a distance, we unconsciously raise our eyebrows slightly and briefly to show that we are pleased to see them: they in turn unconsciously recognise this sign of friendship. We also lift our eyebrows to express a wide range of emotions including pleasure, attraction and sympathy.

Interestingly, dogs have also developed this skill. They raise their eyebrows to make themselves look more appealing to their owners. They seem to know that this will help to ensure their place in the family group. Did they copy us? We don't know but it is possible as dogs have been companions to humans and have lived in close proximity with us for thousands of years. They've certainly had plenty of time to develop and perfect this handy skill.

Word of mouth

Our mouths can be relied upon to express our pleasures, our tensions and our discomforts and they will even indicate when we disagree with something or someone. Clenching our teeth is a sign of tension. Biting or pulling on our lower lip is a comforting gesture, useful when we are anxious or under pressure. It takes us back to the security we experienced when we were tiny suckling infants. We may feel a need to bite or pull on our lower lip if, for example, we are watching an exciting game of football, a nail biting (another comfort gesture) tennis match, a scary thriller on TV, or we've been asked a question to which we are struggling to find the answer.

When we feel miserable and sad we turn our mouths down and, of course, this gesture itself can make us feel sad. If we disagree with someone or something we may well compress (tighten) or purse our lips. These gestures tend to be automatic and over time they may well become entrenched.

One expression that is generally viewed as rude and cheeky is the wonderfully expressive 'poking your tongue out' gesture beloved of small children. With a long tradition and well-deserved reputation for being bawdy and ribald, it can also be a taunt, can be provocative and can even express disgust. It is difficult to pin down the origins of this gesture although there is a reference to it as a taunt as far back as the Old Testament. It is probably even older.

We can create a more pronounced version of the tongue poking if we push our tongue out fully and down and open our mouth and eyes wide. This turns the cheeky expression into an aggressive one. This is a universally understood gesture, one that signals war and warning. It too is ancient and can even be observed in other primates.

It would hardly be stretching the truth to say that the most important gesture we possess is our smile. A smile will take us a long way in any interaction but especially if we want to ask a question, make a point, diffuse aggression, create harmony or encourage others. Our smile is also the most visible and the easiest of our facial expressions to recognise. This is no accident. The smile is the major signal that indicates to others that we are friendly. When shown a series of pictures of people either smiling or not smiling, most of us will judge those who are smiling as more familiar and more honest and trustworthy than those who are not smiling.

Interestingly, the smile is also one of our most versatile gestures. We don't have just one smile. Indeed, we have around twenty smiles and we take out whichever smile is the right one for the occasion, using each as needed in a variety of situations. Here are just three examples from our stock of smiles.

The polite smile, sometimes called the social smile, is our default smile, the one we use most often and the one we pull out of stock when needed. When we adopt the polite smile our lips are usually closed and the smile doesn't reach our eyes. It's an automatic smile and the easiest smile to fake. We might use it when we greet someone new. We want to appear friendly and create a good impression but at the same time we are reluctant to give away too much about ourselves until we know them a little better. It's also the smile we bring out to engage with someone we don't particularly like. The polite smile is a mask behind which we can hide our emotions and is particularly useful if we are feeling anxious.

The two-faced smile, so called because it passes two conflicting messages, is a dishonest smile. We know instinctively that when we see someone smiling at us it should mean that they are friendly, but there is something about this smile that leads us to suspect that this isn't the case. It looks just a little too much like a smirk; the mouth is pulled back with the lips closed and the chin slightly raised. The two-faced smile has no intention of reaching the eyes. The two-faced smile is the smile of smugness, the smile of arrogance and superiority. It is a put down; it is dismissive and aggressive. When we are unlucky enough to be on the receiving end of it we are likely to feel uncomfortable although we may not necessarily know why.

The genuine smile is impossible to misinterpret. It's not forced in any way and our whole face lights up. Our lips are parted and wide, our teeth are visible. The smile reaches our eyes. If you look closely at the genuine smile you will see those tiny laughter lines at the outer edges of each eye.

Before we humans learned to speak we were already well skilled in communicating with each other through our facial expressions and it may be the case that learning to move our facial muscles to form a smile helped us on the road to spoken language. The natural scientist Charles Darwin certainly thought so. He was the first to record the different meanings of the smile and he saw this range of facial expression as an important step on the language-learning continuum.

TRY THIS

Stand in front of a mirror and try out each of the three smiles you have just read about. Note how your eyes remain dull with the polite smile. Note whether your chin automatically rises slightly with the two-faced smile. Note how the genuine smile makes your eyes sparkle. Which is the smile you use most often?

Our smile has its roots in appeasement. Juvenile chimpanzees will smile in the presence of an older dominant male as a way of showing deference. Chimpanzees will also smile to express fear and to diffuse aggression. We too will sometimes smile to indicate deference and to diffuse aggression. We may smile when faced with unpleasantness, to smooth things over and to promote harmony. Surprisingly, just like chimpanzees, we even smile when we are feeling embarrassed, anxious or frightened. Our anxious smile performs the same role as the nervous laugh. They are both rational, appeasing responses to a perceived threat. It does seem that when it comes to the smile we may not be so very different from those chimpanzees; they are, after all our close relatives.

Peoples across the whole world smile. Again, it was Charles Darwin who first made the observation that people in every society in the world appear to smile to indicate pleasure and happiness. This universality suggests that the smile is innate, that we are born already knowing how to smile. When you pick up your new baby or grandchild and smile at her she may well copy you and smile back at you. You may think that you have shown her how to smile but she already knows how to do it. Babies smile even before they are born when they hear a human voice and babies who are born blind smile.

Another interesting aspect of the smile is that we seem to be hardwired to smile back when another person smiles at us. If a stranger were to smile at us as they passed us in the street, our default response would be to smile back at them. We can override this default setting but we have to think about it. Just like a number of our other gestures, including yawning and laughing, the smile appears to be contagious.

TRY THIS

Smile at someone and note how they respond to you. You may not wish to smile at a complete stranger, but have a go at smiling at someone you perhaps know a little. This could be someone who works in the same building as you, those people you pass occasionally and wouldn't normally greet, or perhaps people who live near to you or use the same shops. How many of them return your smile?

EMOTIONS

It was Charles Darwin who first recognised the similarity between the way animals and humans express their emotions through their bodies, noting that expressions of joy and pain in the faces of apes were mirrored by humans. Darwin was also the first to suggest that many of our facial expressions are innate and that our ability to recognise them is also inherited and universal. Current wisdom leans towards Darwin's theories by providing evidence that we do not typically learn specific emotional expressions by copying others when we are young.

It would appear to be an awesome task to catalogue this multiplicity of expressions that our faces are able to convey. Nevertheless, in 1975 the American psychiatrist Paul Ekman identified and recorded the following six emotions that we express in our faces.

anger disgust surprise interest sadness happiness.

Ekman suggested that these six expressions are recognised by just about everyone in the world and so considered them to be universal, thus supporting Darwin's theory. Universal gestures tend to be those that are more automatic and instinctive rather than learned and just like the smile, these emotional gestures are likely to be innate.

Here are likenesses to Ekman's original six expressions. Can you match the six emotions with these six faces?

It is now generally accepted that our faces can convey a much wider range of emotions than these original six although there are numerous grey areas between the different emotions. We can also easily express combined emotions and even contradictory, combined emotions, for example, 'happily disgusted' or 'sadly angry'. (To find out more Google: Ekman et al ' Facial Expression Recognition'.)

TRY THIS

Think of an occasion when you couldn't find something you really needed, perhaps your car keys. You put them down somewhere and then, when you needed to use your car, your keys were nowhere to be seen. Imagine for a moment what was going through your mind. What were your thoughts? And more importantly how might you have been feeling?

Perhaps the thoughts going through your mind were along the lines of, 'Where on earth did I put them? They should be in my coat pocket/handbag and they're just not there. How am I going to get to work without the car?' The feelings that accompanied those thoughts were likely to be puzzlement perhaps, or frustration and possibly a lurking fear that the keys might have gone for good.

Did you feel your face changing as those thoughts and feelings passed through your mind? Did your mouth tighten a little, did you frown, bite your bottom lip, look upwards or sigh; or something else? Your face could have made any of these changes or all of them. Just like when we talk to ourselves, this is a conversation you have with yourself; the only difference is it is your face that is doing the talking. We find it just about impossible not to express our emotions through our faces and it doesn't even matter whether there is anyone else around to witness the event.

MOTIVATIONS AND INTENTIONS

This ambiguity of emotions that we can express illustrates the difficulty of identifying what a particular gesture might actually mean. Indeed, when we interact with other people in our day-to-day lives we don't look at or interpret any one specific gesture in isolation but we take in the whole picture; in other words what someone's whole body is telling us.

Having said this, some expressions are easier to interpret than others. Take for example, what we might do if we say something we wish we hadn't, something we wish we could take back. This is the social gaffe, that 'oops' moment when we probably want to use our hands to push those words back into our mouths or better still, cover our mouth to prevent them from spilling out in the first place. But it's too late. Those embarrassing words are there in the open for anyone to hear. Yet our bodies cannot quite believe this has happened and they try their best to put a stop on things to limit the damage. Children do this quite openly. If they say something silly their hand will go straight to cover their mouth in an attempt to keep the words in. Adults rarely do this. Once we reach adulthood we become more skilled at camouflaging this gesture yet we can still find it difficult to keep our hands away from our mouths. Most adults who have made a gaffe will camouflage the hand to mouth movement with a stroke of the mouth or chin, a scratch to the side of the cheek or convert it into a coughing gesture.

More difficult to identify than the social gaffe are those facial gestures that will tell us that we are being lied to. Sometimes it is the hand to mouth gesture that might indicate that someone is telling a lie. Experienced liars will be unlikely to use this gesture but they might still find it difficult to prevent a hand making its way to the face or the side of the head.

Success in spotting a lie takes considerable experience of dealing with liars. Police officers who have experience of interviewing suspected criminals might say that they can sometimes tell when someone is lying if their body language and their words contradict each other, especially if their body language suddenly changes. For example, they may be happy making eye contact and then when asked a certain question look away.

Police officers, customs officers and poker players will usually score highly at picking out the liars. If you were to ask them how they do it they are likely to put their success down to gut feeling. What those police officers, customs officers and poker players are doing when they tell you they have a gut feeling about someone they suspect of telling a lie is delving into a rich mental store of experience developed over many years of dealing with liars. When they reach into that mental store of experience they are unconsciously processing thousands of tiny expressions that they have witnessed on the faces of liars in the past.

These tiny expressions, sometimes called micro-expressions, are fleeting, barely visible facial expressions. They come in a variety of forms. They could for example be lifted eyebrows, tightened lips, nodding, shaking the head from side to side, blinking, and a whole range of eye movements.

Eye movements need special mention here as they are often seen as a give away for the liar; hence the description of the liar as 'shifty eyed'. These eye movements could include staring, looking up or down, or looking to one side or the other, or even darting about. Whilst any of these could mean a lie none of them necessarily does so and may well indicate something completely different such as concentrating hard, searching memory for a particular piece of information, discomfort or lack of confidence.

One point of interest is whether someone suspected of lying is looking to their left or their right. Although a far from foolproof indication of lying it can indicate whether someone is more likely to be imagining or recalling. Looking to the right taps in to the more creative, emotional side of the brain whereas looking to the left, the more factual side of the brain and to our memory.

A number or cluster of micro-expressions might well indicate a lie. Sometimes the micro-expressions are not new expressions as such; they can be expressions that the person would use anyway but, if they are being deceitful, they might use them more, or even less often, for example they might nod or blink more or less often than usual. This is one reason why it is usually easier to work out whether someone is lying when you know them well; you already have experience of their typical expressions.

WHERE ARE WE NOW?

» Our faces are unique to us: they are capable of conveying an almost limitless variety of expressions that can be recognised and understood by others.
» We have a stock of smiles that we dip into as required: the smile is universal and has it roots as an appeasement gesture.
» Some expressions are easier to interpret than others, but it is not possible to say that a particular expression has a specific meaning.
» It is not easy to tell when someone is telling a lie: it takes considerable experience of observing the micro-expressions on the face of a person who may be lying.

When we interpret the meanings expressed in faces of those around us we do so by looking at the whole picture; that is by observing their facial expressions in unison with the rest of their body. Yet there is one more vital player in this scenario, the role that our voice plays in our every interaction. This is the theme of the following chapter.

3

MORE THAN WORDS:
WHY SPEAKING NEEDS A LITTLE HELP

Are you a fan of the ever popular Dr Who TV series? Mention Dr Who and immediately it is the Daleks that jump into your mind, those sinister aliens who set out to conquer the universe and rid it of all inferior races. As far as the Daleks were concerned that meant all races apart from Daleks! So well known have these aliens become that 'Dalek' even has an entry in the Oxford dictionary. Scary though their appearance was to millions of impressionable youngsters (and many of their parents) it was their voices that really planted terror into countless hearts and minds with their orders to 'Exterminate! Exterminate!'

The creators of the Daleks were pretty successful in giving them a voice that was alien, harsh, terrifying and pitiless and most important of all devoid of any emotion. They did it by manufacturing an electronic voice that was staccato, without rhythm and unchanging in pitch and tone. With these simple adjustments they created a voice that was as far removed from the human voice as was possible. Far removed because it is those very facets that allow us to produce the diverse and nuanced sounds we make every time we speak, those sounds that enable us to convey our every emotion.

This chapter explores this diversity of sound that we make whenever we speak. It looks at how we are able to produce such a multiplicity of sounds, at the rhythm of speaking and at what our voices are actually able to convey. It then looks at the relationship between speaking, our facial expressions and our gestures.

A MULTIPLICITY OF SOUNDS

When we speak we make it appear effortless but speaking requires a complex orchestration of various participants. Every time we open our mouths we are using around half a million of our brain cells. These cells are found in the language centres of our brain and they take up a huge amount of the space here. As a matter of interest, for most most right-handed people the language centre is in the left side of the brain. This is the side that controls the right side of the body. The right side of the brain specialises in visual spatial skills and controls the left side of the body. For most left-handers it's the other way round, although some left-handed people use the left side or both sides.

TRY THIS

The next time you are listening to someone speaking try repeating what they are saying as they are speaking to you. You don't need to do it aloud, just in your head will do. At the same time tap with one of the fingers of your right hand. Then repeat this same tap but this time tap with one of the fingers of your left hand.

Did you find it more difficult to tap with your right finger than your left finger? If you did, and most of us do because most of us are right-handed, it is because your right finger is competing with the available language space in the left hemisphere of your brain.

It makes sense that speaking requires so many of our brain cells when you consider what these brain cells need to do. They are responsible for setting in motion a hugely complex process. Clearly, it involves making sure that we successfully locate from our language memory store the words we have in mind to say. Yet speaking requires more than finding the right words. It requires the actual sounds to be vocalised alongside and separate from the words we choose to use. It isn't easy to think of the sound of our voice separately from the words we use because we are so used to them working as a single unit. Yet those brain cells are engaged in mustering over a hundred muscles of the vocal tract, mouth and face to produce a rich diversity of sound. And as you will see later in this chapter, when we speak our voices have a separate and important role to play.

Perhaps the first thing to consider about our voice is how it works, the mechanics of producing the sounds we make. One important point to note is that all sound is movement; we create the sound of our voice by getting our vocal cords to vibrate. This process begins with our diaphragm, that powerful muscle that stretches across our chest beneath our lungs. We use our diaphragm to push air up from our lungs and through our larynx or voice box. This air causes the vocal cords inside the larynx to vibrate and it is this vibration that produces the sound of our voice. You can prove for yourself that the sound of your voice is created by the vibration of your vocal cords.

TRY THIS

1. Place the thumb and two fingers of one hand lightly and gently either side of your neck at the level of your larynx; it can be found roughly between the bottom of your ears and the top of your shoulders about half way down your neck.

2. Push air out through your mouth as if you are hissing. As you do this you should feel nothing, no movement, no vibration. This is because you are not engaging your vocal cords and so you're not producing actual sound.

3. Now keep your fingers in place and this time make the buzzing sound of a bee, the sound of ZZZZ. You will now be able to feel the vibration of your vocal cords because you are now making sound.

The sounds that we produce from the vibrations of our vocal cords pass up through our vocal tract, resonating through our mouths. This allows us to produce a vast array of sounds that we can vary and adjust to suit a variety of interactive encounters. This whole process involves engaging not only the diaphragm but also the muscles of the vocal tract itself, including those of our mouth and tongue and our face. Working in harmony these muscles enable us to create our spectacular range of sounds.

The next time you are in conversation with someone focus your attention on listening to the sound of their voice rather than the words themselves. Notice how their voice changes as they speak. You may notice changes in the tone of their voice, in its pitch, its volume or its pace. You may notice pauses in their speech and that the speaker emphasises specific words and phrases.

TONE

Our tone of voice is really a description of the quality of our individual voice. We may naturally have a deep voice, or it might be harsh, or clear, or strong, or soft; we might even own a gravelly voice. In fact, our voice is unique to us. Each of us has a voice that is distinctive and different from anyone else, so much so that its sound can be used as a means of identity. Additionally, our tone of voice has some bearing on the way others perceive us. This is because tone is also about the way we use our voice. We may for example soften it to express warmth or sympathy and harden it when we feel annoyed.

PITCH

The pitch of our voice describes its high or low frequency, a little like the Do Re Mi on a musical scale. We may well use a higher pitch if we are feeling uncertain about what we are saying; perhaps we are asking for directions or checking things out. We usually raise the pitch at the end of a sentence if we are asking a question and lower it when we are making a point. We may also use a lower pitch that then drops at the end of a phrase or sentence to produce an authoritative, commanding voice.

VOLUME

We may increase the volume when we are making a point or when we are feeling annoyed and decrease it when we are sharing confidences, supporting or consoling someone or when we are talking about something private or sensitive.

PACE

We are easily able to control the pace of our voice, slowing it down when we are expressing sympathy or concern and increasing it when we are conveying something interesting or exciting, or we are making a point. We can also use pauses to slow down the pace, if for example we are explaining something, perhaps describing the intricate plot of a book or film that we have enjoyed. Sometimes we will slow the pace to emphasise a particular aspect of what we are saying, for example we might pause before the punch-line when telling a joke. At other times we pause if we want time to consider what we are going to say next or we are feeling nervous.

BACKING GROUP

Our voices have their own backing group. This backing group includes coughs, sighs, groans and laughter, as well as sounds such as 'um', 'er', 'oh' and 'ah'. This backing group comes in handy when we want time to think; we are not sure what we want to say and need to consider which words we will use. These backing performers can become a habit and you may know someone who has a habitual cough or laugh. Both the cough and the laugh can have nervous origins. The nervous laugh especially has its roots as an appeasement gesture, to smooth things over and works in much the same way as the nervous smile.

THE RHYTHM OF SPEAKING

When we use our voices to broadcast our words we are, in essence, playing music, the music of language. We have what has been termed rhythm ability. This begins before we are even born when we hear the sound of our mother's heartbeat. Language, especially spoken language has its own rhythm and we latch on to it. This is how we learn to speak it and to understand it. When we hear people talking we hear the rhythm in their voices and our brain responds to this because of the shared neural pathways in the brain between language and rhythm. We respond to the rhythm inherent in the sound of someone speaking in a remarkably similar way that we respond

to the beat in music. Indeed, children who experience difficulties with learning language can be helped by exposure to musical rhythm. This relationship between language and rhythm is likely to be one reason why parents sing lullabies and recite nursery rhymes to their babies and toddlers. (To find out more Google: Fujii S & Wan C 'The role of rhythm in speech and language rehabilitation'.)

There is also a strong neural connection between speaking and listening. The brain cells that control our mouths when we speak are the very same cells that can be activated when we listen to spoken language. Whilst you are listening to someone speaking these brain cells are busy miming the words you are hearing.

FACTS, FEELINGS AND JUDGEMENTS

Our voices perform two important jobs for us. The first is to convey the hard facts of what we say and the second is to allow us to express our emotions. We can easily use our voice to change the facts of what we say without making any changes to the words we use. Here are a couple of examples for you to try out.

TRY THIS

1. You can give the following sentence seven different factual meanings as you use your voice to place the emphasis in turn, on each of the seven words it contains.

I never said she stole my money

2. Take the following phrase.

Shut the door

This is a short, straightforward statement to convey the fact that we wish a door to be closed. By emphasising the word 'shut' and lowering the pitch of your voice you can change it into a command and by raising the pitch at the end you can convert it into a request.

Try saying 'shut the door' to mean: 'Are you sure you want the door shut?' Note the changes in your voice.

Now say it to mean 'Is it the door you want shut?' (rather than, for example, the window). Note the changes in your voice.

We are well skilled in using our voices in this way. Yet our ability to pass and change the factual content of our messages, as you did just now, is surpassed by the second of the two jobs our voice performs for us. This is its supreme skill in passing the emotional content of our messages, to tell others how we are feeling. Have another look at that phrase 'shut the door' but now consider how you might express the emotion of being fed up.

TRY THIS

Imagine that the door is constantly being left open. You are feeling cold. You are also feeling angry and exasperated as everyone, apart from you, forgets to close it. Now say 'shut the door' to show that you feel completely fed up and note the sound of your voice.

You probably spoke slowly, your words embellished with an extended sigh. Our voices are especially adept at conveying our emotions and they usually do the job far better than our spoken words. And just like expressing our emotions through our body, when we express them through our voice we generally do it unconsciously. For example, in a stressful situation our voice is likely to express our feelings of anxiety. It may become unsteady, weak and shaky, although we may not necessarily be aware of these changes.

If we are able to convey and change facts and feelings through the sound of our voice as we are speaking, those listening to us are equally able to glean a host of information about us from just listening to the sound of our voice. It's usually reasonably easy for others to tell whether we are male or female, youngish or older and they may also be able to detect our background, possibly where we were brought up, our education and so on. Perhaps less obvious is that they will also use the sound of our voice to make judgements about our character, for example, to decide whether we are trustworthy, sincere, credible, kind, attractive, and so on – or not!

A Dazzling Triple Act

Whenever we speak to one another we are taking advantage of an alliance that exists between our spoken words, our voice and our bodies. Only with the expressions on our face will our words and our voice convey the complete picture of what we are saying. This can be illustrated when you think about what happens when we read an exciting or frightening story aloud. Not only do we use our voice to accentuate the excitement or the fear in the story but, as we speak, we alter our facial expression, automatically adopting an animated or frightening expression when appropriate, perhaps widening our eyes or pulling our lips back.

Our hands and arms also play their part in supporting the sound of our voice and our words. In the previous chapter you saw how just about every one of us will use them to express ourselves when we speak and that these gestures help us to regulate the pace and the rhythm of our spoken words. Yet there is more to this relationship between speaking and gesture than the regulation of pace and rhythm.

Try this

For this you need an assistant, someone who will listen to you while you say something to them. You can do this on your own and just pretend someone is listening to you but this doesn't give you quite the same experience as you have if you do it with a listener. Nor is it as much fun.

You are going to spend just one minute giving your listener some directions. It matters not a jot where you direct them. Possibilities include going from your home to the local shops or the nearest bar, or from your work place desk to the photocopier, the toilets or somewhere else. What you need to do is to visualise the route they will have to follow and then to describe aloud each step they will need to take. There is, however, just one important point before you start, something you need to keep in mind the whole time you are speaking. You must not use your hands. You need to keep them absolutely still the whole time. You may find it easier to sit on them. Now, go ahead and say aloud the directions you have visualised.

How did you get on? Did you find it difficult to keep your hands still? Did you find you wanted to point to left or right with your shoulders to indicate turning a corner or nod your head to indicate going ahead? Did you want to raise your chin, to indicate going up a hill or stairs? If you did you are not alone. We instinctively use our hands, and indeed other parts of our bodies to gesture as we speak and we can find it disconcerting to speak without our bodies being involved. If you are naturally more expressive with your hands and arms you will have found this task even more difficult.

There is a good reason why most of us find it immensely difficult to speak without using our hands and arms. It is because our spoken words and our gestures are connected; some of the neural pathways in our brains for language and for gestures are shared. Using gestures when we speak enables our brains to sort what we are going to say into a logical order. In other words, our gestures help us to think clearly when we speak. How does this work? As we move our hands and arms around we create a picture to illustrate our words. Someone might for example, ask you about your new sports car or racing bike and as you respond verbally your hands will begin to draw a picture of said car or bike. The pictures we create with our hands and arms help us to articulate our words. This picture is also available to our listener and will help them to get a better idea of what we are talking about. Using gestures when we speak is especially useful when we are explaining something complex. (To find out more Google: McNeill D 'Hand and Mind: 'What gestures reveal about thought'.)

As a point of interest, using gestures when we speak can influence how our listener may judge us and what we are saying. As a general rule, when we use gestures other people are likely to see us as more effective and competent. Gestures also help us to persuade and influence others; this could be useful in an interview situation. However, the gestures we use do need to be genuine. (To find out more Google: Koppensteiner M & Grammar K 'Perceiving Personality in Simple Motion Cues'.)

Interestingly, although our hand and arm gestures support and reinforce our spoken words, this relationship doesn't work in reverse; concentrating on the words we are using will inhibit our gestures. You can see this in action when you watch a talk show programme on the TV. When the interviewer is in conversation with one of their guests they will use their hands as they speak but, on the whole, when they turn to face the audience, use the autocue and concentrate on reading the words, their hands become still.

Our words, our voice and our bodies are, in truth, a dazzling triple act. They operate as a whole, seamlessly and effortlessly. At first appearance this harmony is surprising because, as you will see in a later chapter, these three evolved, not as one, but separately. Yet it is as if these three were born to work together; all the members of this superb cast perform in harmony to produce a star performance.

The students receiving their exam results that were mentioned in the introduction to this section on body language illustrate what happens in this triple act performance. The students who did well in their exams will be broadcasting their immense pleasure. They will do this through spoken words, for example, 'It's awesome, brilliant, fantastic.' They will do it through their voices; rapid, high pitched and perhaps interspersed with squeals of delight. And they will do it through their bodies; broad grins, arms up and out and sometimes jumping up and down. For those students who did not achieve the results they wanted, the picture is different. They may voice their feelings as spoken words, for example, 'I'm really disappointed' but their feelings of disappointment would certainly be evident in their voice; dull and slow and in their bodies; glum face and hunched shoulders.

This triple alliance between our spoken words, our voice and our body is one where our voice and body have the final say. An example to illustrate is when our voice and our body pass a message that is different from our words. Say, for example, we are worried about a problem. A friend might ask us if we are OK. If we then reply that we are fine when our voice and our face are clearly showing that we are not, it will be our voice and face that are taken note of rather than our words. We can also use our voice and body to deliberately contradict our words.

TRY THIS

Stand in front of a mirror and give yourself a compliment. You might say something like 'Don't you look great this morning?' or 'I like that shirt, tie, hairstyle'. Next, repeat the compliment but this time, use your voice and body to turn it into a sarcastic comment. Note how your expression changes and note the change in your voice.

There is more to this story of the harmony and sometimes disharmony between our words, our voice and our body: this triple act is only part of the picture that illustrates our interactions. As you will see in later chapters the business of interacting with each other is as nuanced as it is intricate.

Where are we now?

» We make speaking appear effortless but it is a complex process that requires us to engage a huge proportion of our brain power.

» Our voices are immensely skilled at conveying and changing not only the facts of what we say but the myriad emotions that are present whenever we speak: our faces provide an extra visual layer that helps us to get our messages across.

» Our hand gestures support our spoken words; these gestures are controlled by the same part of the brain that controls spoken language and they assist by creating a picture of spoken language. When we listen to someone speaking our brain mimes the words we hear. We have rhythm ability; we recognise and tune in to the rhythm in language.

» Our spoken words, our voice and our bodies perform a dazzling triple act to help us to get our messages across to others.

To capture the complete picture of the relationship between our words, our voice and our body language and to work out why these three co-operate so well we need explore spoken language itself. But before we do that we will delve a little deeper into the origins and evolution of our body language. This is the theme of the next chapter.

4

FIGURATIVELY SPEAKING: WHY OUR BODIES SPEAK

How can you tell when an animal is frightened? If you have a dog or a cat you will certainly know. Even if you're not a pet owner the chances are that you will have seen a cowering dog, its body lowered, its ears back and its tail down, or a cat with its body arched and its fur on end. And you'll easily recognise a happy and joyful dog when its tail is wagging and its ears are up.

Animals don't have spoken language but they share with us a talent for talking to each other and to us through their bodies. So where did their body language and indeed ours originate, and is there a connection between the two? This chapter looks back at the origins of body language, how it came about and when it first appeared in our species. It offers an explanation for why we use our bodies to speak to each other and then goes on to explore two vital jobs that body language does: supporting our spoken words and expressing our emotions.

How did it begin

What is the story behind our body language? When and how did we learn to use our bodies to talk to each other? We don't know all the answers but the ones we do know are surprising and compelling. Taking the 'when' question first, we know that we have been using our bodies to communicate for a very long time, far longer than we have been using spoken language.

Suppose we imagine a timeline to record events. Let's say one end of the time line is our modern era and the other end six million years ago. This is a useful starting point because it is around this time that we humans diverged from other primates and began to evolve into our human species. Now we know that chimpanzees use a complex and often human like system of body signals to communicate with each other. For example a chimp will use an open hand gesture to ask for food from another chimp. This is very similar to the universal human gesture of begging for food or alms. So we can say with some confidence that body language has been around in our species for at least six million years.

But is six million years the starting point? Or do we need to go back further than this? To find the answer consider for a moment how easily and effortlessly we use our bodies to communicate. Have you ever thought how automatic and unconscious it is? It seldom appears on our radar; it just happens. This is a clue that points us a long way back, in fact far back beyond our divergence from other primates, back to the animal kingdom. We know that animals communicate through body language so we need to go back a long way, possibly tens of millions of years.

Focusing on the animal kingdom also gives us some answers to the question of how we began to communicate through our bodies. How do these other animals communicate with each other? One way they have is by smell. We can't do this because our noses are too small. But animals have another trick up their sleeves. They are very good at observing and in particular observing potential predators. They are alert, not just for the appearance of a potential predator, but alert to what the predator might be intending to do. They are looking at the predator's body, searching for any signs that would give away its intentions. There's a lot at stake here. If you could read the minds of these observant animals it is likely their thoughts would be something along the lines of 'What is this predator going to do? Is it going to eat me? Do I need to make a quick getaway?' Many animal species are exceptionally skilled at observing and interpreting the body signals of potential predators. (To find out more Google: Gustafson L 'Speaking Up: The Origins of Language' TED talk.)

Now the predators are not aware that they are broadcasting their intentions to their potential prey. The messages they are passing via their bodies are unintentional. Over an extended period of time some of these unintentional messages may well have evolved to become intentional or deliberate. These intentional messages can be seen in a number of primate communities. Chimpanzees in particular are very observant. An alpha male might make an aggressive facial gesture; subordinate chimpanzees will observe it and know how to respond appropriately, perhaps with an appeasement gesture such as bowing low or smiling. (To find out more Google: Hobaiter C 'Chimpanzee Language: Communication gestures translated'.)

Many of the gestures that can be observed in chimps can also be observed in our human species. The appeasing smile is a recognisable example that we share with chimpanzees, but we have developed and refined these body signals over the six or so million years of our evolution.

Imagine the following scenario. Two strangers find themselves in a room together. There is no one else around. Neither of them speaks the other's language. Pretty soon something interesting happens. They begin a conversation with each other but it is a conversation without words. The first thing that is likely to happen is that one will make an exploratory approach through eye contact, searching out the possibility of a connection. The other will most likely respond in kind and then perhaps offer a tentative smile. Emboldened by the experience, perhaps one would hold out their arm in a gesture that means 'Hello' or invite the other to shake their hand. All of these gestures, the eye contact, smiles and the handshakes are communicating friendly intentions. They are speaking to each other through their bodies and they are speaking a universal language.

Our sophisticated system of communicating with each other through our bodies has enabled us to connect with each other, to use our bodies to signal our intentions and most importantly to signal our friendly intentions. This ability to express friendship is likely to have allowed us to join together to form strong, protective, co-operative groups and increase our chances of survival.

It does seem to be the case that the origins of our body language are ancient, beginning life as unintentional signals in the animal kingdom. Using our bodies as a way of connecting to others is certainly one of its major missions but body language has numerous other tasks to perform.

A PERSONAL ASSISTANT PAR EXCELLENCE

We have a perfectly good spoken language so you might wonder why we humans, once we began to speak, didn't just dispense with the body language as surplus to requirements. You might expect that this would have been the case but it just didn't happen. Notwithstanding our ongoing attachment to communicating through our bodies, it has to be said that before our ancient ancestors learned to speak, they were far better than we modern humans at both expressing and reading each other's body signals. This does make sense if this was the only way they were able to communicate with each other.

Yet it was vital for our species to retain this ability. This is because body language has an important role as a personal assistant to spoken language, organising and managing the whole process of speaking. If you were to compile a job description to cover its duties it would need to include regulating speaking, emphasising some words over others and standing in for words whenever it was required to do so. The job clearly requires a Jack-of-all-trades and our bodies easily fit the bill because they are already so well experienced at communicating.

Regulating our speaking is carried out in a whole range of ways. Even in a very simple conversation our body language manages the way the conversation is played out. For example, maintaining eye contact during conversation confirms to both participants that the speaker will continue to speak and the listener continue to listen. On the other hand, if one participant looks away this is a signal for a change. As listeners we will also use other signals to show that we are interested in what we are hearing and wish the speaker to continue. For example, we may lean forward, nod our head or raise our eyebrows.

Talking to each other has been likened to participating in a dance. It is a dance that is choreographed by our body language. It is also a dance that we know very well; we know when to enter the dance, when to exit and we know all of its intricate steps and movements.

Try this

When you are next in conversation with someone, a friend, a family member, a work colleague or even an everyday interaction in a shop, take a moment to observe the other participant in your conversation. Look at what their body is doing. Note when they make eye contact with you and when they look away as they speak and listen. Note whether they smile and nod in agreement. Watch their hands as they speak and notice how and when they alter their body position.

Emphasising words that we feel are important is an ongoing job carried out easily by our bodies, mainly though changes in our voice and our facial expression but our hands and arms also play their part. We choose to emphasise certain words to make them mean more than they would on their own. Imagine the angler telling friends about 'the one that got away'. You can see him with his hands spread wide to either side of his body and his face and voice animated as he tells you that the fish that he almost caught was 'this' big. You know for sure that this fish would have been much smaller without this gesture.

Now imagine you have just eaten a delicious piece of chocolate cake and you are asked whether you enjoyed it. You close your eyes, tip your chin up and give a satisfied smile. Or think about an occasion where you are listening to someone talking enthusiastically and excitedly about a particular topic; the chances are that their hands and arms will be moving rapidly and excitedly to express their enthusiasm.

Sometimes we need our bodies to stand in for our words. When called on to take over this all-important duty our body will take up the slack instantly and effortlessly. Perhaps it's a situation where it is inconvenient for us to speak. For example, you might see some friends across the road but it is too far, or too noisy with traffic sounds for you to shout 'Hi' so you wave to them instead. Or perhaps you are in a cake shop and want to buy one of those delicious chocolate cakes behind the counter. The assistant asks which cake you want and so you use your finger to point to it. Sometimes we are just feeling lazy; we are asked a question, we are not sure of the answer and we shrug our shoulders because we cannot be bothered to respond with words.

There are other reasons why we might choose to use our body rather than words to say something. Consider the small child who is reluctant to go to school. You observe his eyes downcast, his bottom lip rolled down clearly telling you, 'I don't want to go to school today!' Or perhaps her head is up, she is grim faced with her arms folded in front of her. There's no doubt in your mind that her message to you is, 'I won't go to school today!'

There are even occasions when using our body rather than words has unexpected advantages; it is far easier to send coded messages this way. You can indicate to a colleague or friend that you wish to leave the boring party or the tedious meeting. Using body language to send a coded message is also handy, though hardly ethical, when playing cards.

EXPRESSING OUR EMOTIONS

Many of the responses our bodies make are intentional and deliberate; shaking hands is an obvious example. On the whole these intentional responses are rational ones; we know that we intend to shake hands with someone. These responses arise in the modern, thinking part of our brain. They also tend to be learned responses, learned from those around us – parents, siblings, friends and so on – and may well vary between communities and cultures. On the other hand, countless numbers of our responses are made automatically and unknowingly, for example touching our face or hair when we feel anxious or putting our hand to our temple when we are thinking.

Consider again those early days in the evolution of body language, the unintentional body signals of those predators. It seems that we still retain and exhibit a vast array of these early unintentional signals that predators display. These unintentional responses are instinctive rather than learned and they tend to be controlled by a far older, more primitive part of our brains. This means that they are far more likely to be shared by just about everyone on this earth. And there is another striking difference between these unintentional responses and our deliberate responses. They are far more likely to be driven by our emotions.

A good example to illustrate this is when we are feeling anxious; we may use gestures designed to make us feel calmer and less fearful. We might, for example use a finger to gently rub our forehead, face or side of the head. These soothing gestures take us back to the safety and security of infancy when a parent would perhaps stroke our forehead to comfort us when we were fractious. We might also attempt to mimic the security and comfort of suckling by putting something in our mouth. Sucking or biting our bottom lip or putting cigarettes, pens, almost anything we have handy into our mouth can also provide this comfort.

It isn't always easy to spot the difference between the two types of body responses, the rational and the emotional, because very often the same gesture can be rational and deliberate as well as being emotional and automatic. Suppose, for example, we use our finger to point to that chocolate cake that we see on the counter in the cake shop to indicate that this is our choice. This would be an intentional, rational gesture. We know we want the chocolate cake and although we might feel a certain amount of emotional connection to the chocolate cake in as much as we might desire it ('I do like chocolate cake') this is largely a rational gesture.

Now suppose that later we are involved in a heated discussion. We want to get our point of view across. We are emotionally involved in this discussion. We feel strongly about what we are saying. We know we are in the right and the other person is wrong. In this situation we might use a pointing gesture as we metaphorically ram home our viewpoint. This same gesture that we were fully aware of when we used it to point to the cake may now be one that we are less aware of, one that is more automatic and instinctive. Most importantly this gesture would now be one that was driven by our heightened emotions.

Or bodies excel at expressing our emotions. You saw in chapter two how effectively our face conveys our emotions. We are an extremely social species. We have a great need to connect with other members of our human 'tribe', to feel a part of our human group, to share our ideas and express our emotions. Indeed, the chances are that we wouldn't have survived unless we were able to connect with others. Expressing our emotions through our bodies enables each of us to make this all-important connection. Our bodies do a spectacular job of telling those around us how we are feeling and it does it faster and better than our words could ever aspire to because it is far, far better adapted for this task.

Say, for example, that we are listening to someone who is talking about a topic that fills us with horror. Perhaps they are describing a scary film or they are talking on a topic that has an extreme political philosophy, one that we strongly disagree with. It is just possible that we might say 'I feel horrified about what you are saying' but it is unlikely. What is almost certain however is that our body will be conveying this message loudly and clearly. It would be passed rapidly and effortlessly through a range of signals: a frown perhaps, a grimace, clenched fists, body leaning back or turned slightly away and possibly with arms crossed.

We also find it easier to get the more uncomfortable and difficult to handle feelings across to others though our bodies rather through spoken language. For example, if something has annoyed us, whilst it is possible we might say 'I feel angry', it is far more likely that our anger will be clearly evident in our raised voice, perhaps a scowl, hunched shoulders, tense muscles and so on. Another scenario is when we put a hand to our mouth if we say something silly or embarrassing. Would we actually say 'I feel embarrassed'? Unlikely!

We cannot get away from the fact that our feelings are constantly on display. Even the simple response of listening to someone as they speak to us will convey our feelings of interest (or lack of it) through eye contact and intermittent head nods. In truth, emotions such as interest, enjoyment and enthusiasm are hugely important in all our interactions with others for maintaining good relationships. This process is ongoing at a level we are mostly unaware of. Our responses are instant; our bodies are constantly primed, ready to communicate our feelings even as we are engaged in the business of speaking and listening.

Emotion is an extremely powerful driving force for body language and we have known for a long time about this connection between our feelings and our bodies. Take, for example, a situation when we are distressed or grief stricken; then we may well just curl up into a tight ball. The relationship between our emotions and our bodies was first recorded over one and a half centuries ago by Charles Darwin. We are familiar with Darwin's theory of evolution, recorded in his book 'Origins of the Species', but Darwin also wrote other books, including one entitled, 'The Expression of the Emotions in Man and Animals'. In this book he recorded his observations of both humans and animals expressing their emotions through their bodies.

One example Darwin gives and is beautifully illustrated in his book is of the cat arching its back when threatened and fearful. It does this to make itself look bigger and to show that it is ready for the battle. In taking up this posture the cat is aiming to appear aggressive to whoever or whatever is threatening it. We can express aggression in exactly the same way as the cat.

The soccer player, angry at the referee's decision might place his hands on his hips, elbows pointing out. He is unlikely to realise that, just like the cat, he is making his body look bigger in order to present a strong and aggressive front to the perceived threat.

Our bodies often tell others how we are feeling without our knowledge. If, for example we are concentrating hard on something we find puzzling, perhaps we are shopping on line and the site is particularly troublesome to navigate, our agitation could well appear as a deep frown, tense lips and so on. Our faces in particular are especially good at displaying our feelings, even having an ability to change colour as we experience different emotions. Anger for example can give our foreheads a slightly red tint in the centre and a slightly blue tint at the sides. On the other hand, feelings of happiness can give us red cheeks. It is thought that this may be one reason why some of us use make up; to make us appear happy and positive to others rather than more attractive or younger.

There are even occasions when our bodies will display our feelings without our consent. This can happen even when we are aware of our feelings. Take blushing as an example. Most blushers know when this embarrassing occurrence is likely, usually when they are feeling uncomfortable or embarrassed. They would prefer not to blush yet they can do nothing to prevent their bodies acting against their wishes.

Our bodies do seem to be better than words at conveying emotions but how much better? One estimate suggests that our words may convey as little as 7%, our voice around 38% and our body language as much as 55%. (To find out more Google: Mehrabian, 1971 'Silent Messages')

These are interesting figures. If you add together the figures for voice and body language it looks like a little over 90% of our messages can be passed through our bodies rather than through the words we are using. This isn't necessarily always the case but it is likely to be the case when we are expressing our feelings. In fact Mehrabian's research focused on feelings.

Many of us find Mehrabian's statistics difficult to accept. Perhaps you too are struggling with this. If you are, have a look at this image.

Now imagine that Jo on the left, whose body language is telling you that he feels happy, says 'I'm feeling sad'. Then imagine that Fred, on the right, whose body language is telling you that he feels sad, says 'I'm feeling happy'. Which do you believe, their bodies or their words? Of course, this isn't an exact experiment as you would normally be hearing the words rather than reading them but it will suffice.

Almost everyone who observes this picture decides that the stronger message comes from the images. There is a good reason for this. We take in far more information through our eyes than we do through our ears. And as you read earlier, we do love images. Indeed, we love them so much we even create them in our language, for example when we use idiom and metaphors. Think of the picture that leaps into your head when you consider the phrase, 'a bull in a china shop' or 'it's raining cats and dogs'.

Using our bodies to communicate with each other gives us tremendous flexibility and scope. We are able to use our facial expressions, our gestures and our whole bodies to guide and structure our interactions and conversations, to emphasise, to replace our spoken words and to express our emotions. Over the course of the millions of years that we have evolved into our modern human species we have developed a complex and sophisticated body language system that not only complements our spoken words but enables us to communicate extremely effectively with each other.

» Body language is ancient: many species communicate their intentions through their bodies.
» Some primates use a complex system of body language similar to ours to communicate with each other.
» Our bodies convey both our intentional and unintentional thoughts to others and are skilled at expressing our emotions.
» Our bodies take on the job of personal assistant to our spoken words by organising, emphasising and sometimes replacing them.
» Our expertise at reading other people's body language can help us to identify their intentions and their emotions.

It is hardly surprising that body language has been given the title of universal language. It has allowed us to make connections to others and to express a massive range of messages both rational and emotional. This chapter has explored the evolution of much of our conscious and unconscious body language. Yet there is much more at play here. Powerful though body language can be in communicating our thoughts, intentions and emotions it does not work in isolation. It has a powerful collaborative partner: language. Language is a remarkable facility and one that has brought us tremendous advantages from co-operation and collaboration and one that has done much to ensure our success. Language provides the theme for the four chapters in the second part of this book.

LANGUAGE

There is a somewhat thought-provoking difference between our human species and just about every other species on this earth. It is that we are the only type of human being on this earth. This is odd because just about every other species has numerous varieties. There are around 20,000 different kinds of bees, over 300 kinds of dog and even the whale, the largest of the mammals, has nineteen varieties. Yet we are alone in being the sole exemplar of a human being on this earth. This hasn't always been the case. There have been other humans; at least three others that we know about were around at the same time as us and it is likely there were more. What happened to those other humans? Why are we still here, the sole survivors when they are long gone?

The simple answer is we don't know. At least we don't know for sure. We may have been able to produce better tools or we may have been better at adapting to a changing environment. We might even have bludgeoned the other humans to death. Yet there is another less bloody possibility that could account for our being here whilst those other humans fell by the wayside. Simply, we are still here because we learned to speak to each other. Speaking gave us the means to build on the relationships forged from communicating through our bodies and enabled us to form co-operative groups. And this is not all. Language also brought us immense success. Everything we have and everything we have done is built upon this one thing, our unique ability to communicate with one another through language.

In this second part of the book we move from exploring the role of body language to looking at language itself. The opening chapter offers a close up of the English language and highlights our skills at engaging with it. The next chapter looks at how we decode language, and then focuses on, and challenges, some of the rules and customs that govern it. The following chapter considers some of the reasons that language experts have put forward to account for how and why we might first have begun to speak to each other. The final chapter in this second part is a mini-history of language; it tells the story of its evolution and then focuses on the development of the English language.

5

IT'S ENGLISH – INNIT:
HOW WE GET LANGUAGE TO WORK FOR US

If you take a look at some of those other species that share this earth with us, our fellow mammals, there is one thing you can't fail to notice; it is their toned muscles and strong bodies. You'll also notice that most will have sharp claws, well adapted for surviving in a tough environment. Many also possess strong teeth, ready to take the first bite. Now what about us? What do you see when you look at our human species? How do we compare? Clearly, you can't fail to notice our relative physical weakness. Even if we are fit, lean and spend hours in the gym we need only to look a little closer to see our problem. Our claws are next to useless, our teeth little better and as for our muscles, shall we say they fall a little short. Indeed, even if we were all high-performance athletes, when it comes to the crunch, our physical performance in a tough world would leave much to be desired. We have got to admit it, we come out of this physical comparison with many of our fellow mammal species pretty badly. And yet…!

And yet our success has been spectacular and it may well be that our possession of language has brought about this success. So what can be said about this language, which, for our purposes, is the English language? This is a language that has been created and engineered by us but also formed by luck and circumstance. That being the case, we might wish to ask a pertinent question or two. We might ask, does the English language work for us? Does it do the job it's supposed to? It would be stretching the truth to say that it unfailingly allows us to understand each other yet it does seem to work for most of us most of the time. This is largely because we are immensely skilled at making it work. To be honest, sometimes it astounds me that we do understand each other so well considering the idiosyncratic nature of our language.

Our success is down to our quite incredible ability to interpret language and to create meaning from it, sometimes against all the odds. So, what exactly do we do with it? We do far more than interpret and create meaning from it. In this chapter we will take a close up look at the English language, unearth some of the ways we engage with it, note some of its quirks and observe our skills at manipulating it for our own convenience, satisfaction and enjoyment.

IN A WORD OR TWENTY!

One of the first things you notice about our modern English language is that it has a lot of words. At the barest minimum count you get around 250,000 words. You arrive at this total if you count each verb in its un-conjugated form and you also ignore the technical or scientific words. It also means counting only once those words that have more than one meaning. For example, the word 'lie' can mean an untruth or to lie down, the word 'fair' can mean bright and clear or reasonable. If you were to count every single word in the English language you could say that it has well over a million words to its credit.

Even at the minimum count of 250,000 words it has been suggested that English has around twice the number of words than are found in the French language. And this number is increasing all the time; around 4,000 words are added to English dictionaries every year. English also contains an extraordinary number of synonyms. This is likely to explain why it needs a thesaurus, something few other languages require.

TRY THIS

How many synonyms do you think there are for the word 'drunk'? Ten? Twenty? More?

Did you opt for more than twenty? If so, you'd be correct. Conservative counts suggest that 'drunk' has around 140 synonyms but some counts accredit this word with over 300 synonyms. (You'll find a selection of them at the end of this chapter.) One reason why English has so many synonyms is because, historically, so many of our words have been imported: from Saxon and Scandinavian languages, from Norman French and from Latin and Greek. New words are constantly being added and they can be added in a number of ways.

>> You can add to the word count by shortening words that are already in use: the word 'bike' is short for bicycle and 'pub' is short for public house.

>> We fashion new words by creating portmanteau words, two words put together: 'crowdfunding' and 'carjack' for example.

>> New words can be generated by chopping up two words and then fitting the pieces together. Examples include: 'smog' (smoke and fog) 'docudrama' (documentary and drama), 'dashcam' (dashboard and camera).

>> Prefixes and suffixes are also a handy way to increase word count. Examples include 'deglobalisation' and 'hazardless'.

>> Words such as 'laptop' and 'digitise' are just made up from necessity, often introduced to accommodate new technology.

>> Words may be stolen from another context. One example is the word 'tank', an armoured vehicle employed during World War One. Its name was co-opted from its code name 'water carrier'. (To find out more Google: Water carrier for Mesopotamia.)

>> New words may be added to accommodate changes in our habits and to reflect the social climate. A couple of examples added to the Oxford English Dictionary in 2018 were, 'mansplainer': someone who explains something in a condescending or patronising manner and 'youthquake'. This word was selected by the Oxford dictionaries as the word of the year in 2017. It is a term for a 'significant cultural, political or social change arising from the actions or influence of young people'. The publisher of the dictionary gave the United Kingdom general election of 2015 as an example of a 'youthquake', when young voters flocked to the opposition party.

This diversity in our language has consequences for us whenever we use it. One of these consequences is that it gives us a great choice when deciding what to say. We can for example, choose any of those 140 synonyms for the word 'drunk'. Some words from our vast store are so appealing that we are drawn to voice them the moment we set eyes on them. Here are two examples although, sadly, neither is in general use today. The first is pretty descriptive of its actual meaning, the second a little more obscure.

TRY THIS

Would you like to be given either of these two labels: **slubberdegullion** or **ultracrepidarian**?

Slubberdegullion means worthless, slovenly, loathsome or disgusting. Its origin is unknown but it could have begun life as a 1500's Dutch German word meaning slobber or smear. Ultracrepidarian means a 'know it all'. It describes someone who offers their opinion or advice on topics they know nothing about. The Latin phrase *ultra crepidam* means 'beyond the sole'. One possible story on its origins concerns a Greek painter (from the works of Pliny the Elder) who used it when referring to a cobbler who had criticised his painting of a foot. The cobbler was told to stick to shoemaking.

WORDS INCOGNITO

Something else that you might notice when you take a good look at English is its flexibility, offering us almost unlimited scope to manipulate it. This flexibility provides us with numerous opportunities to use words and phrases that may well mean something completely different from what they actually say. We might choose to do this for different reasons. Here are a few examples.

TRY THIS

Here are three comments you could be unlucky enough to hear from someone. Do you think they mean something different from what they actually say?

'With the greatest respect...'
'I'll bear it in mind'
'You must come for dinner'
(The Independent newspaper 11/11/15)

I'm sure you had no trouble putting your own interpretation on these comments. Here are my suggestions along with The Independent's interpretation in brackets.

1. I am about to disagree entirely with what you are saying. (I think you are an idiot.)
2. I am not interested in what you've said and I probably won't be following it up. (I've forgotten it already.)
3. I've done my duty by inviting you for dinner but you and I know I don't really mean it. (It's not an invitation; I'm just being polite.)

Here is a second example of words that mean something different from what they say.

TRY THIS

Take a look at this mini story.

It had been a dog day. I'd bitten off more than I could chew. Then I'd thrown the baby out with the bathwater. Now I was in hot water.

Did you have any problem working out what the story was about? This is a nonsense story of course. Individually the sentences probably didn't make a lot of sense but I expect you understood the meaning of the story pretty much along the following lines.

Things had been difficult all day. I'd taken on more than I could manage and then I'd ended up dumping some of the really important stuff along with the rubbish. This is going to cause me a lot of problems.

You probably recognised immediately that the story is written in idiom, words and phrases that aren't meant to be taken literally. Not one of the sentences actually means what it says. Our language is jam-packed with idiom; we use it unconsciously and seamlessly whenever we speak and write. And we interpret and understand it effortlessly.

Idiom gives our language its vibrancy and richness, enables speedy interpretation, provides clarity and makes the content more meaningful. It is first and foremost a short cut. Take a look at the phrase 'thrown the baby out with the bathwater'. If you were speaking literally you would need significantly more words to get the meaning over. Idiom allows us to say more with fewer words. You may well have noticed that the first story, told in idiom, was far shorter than the second story (25 words as opposed to 40 words).

Secondly, idiom is a way of passing complex ideas more easily. Take that same phrase 'thrown the baby out with the bathwater' again. With this image in our minds we get a clear idea of something important (the baby) inadvertently or carelessly discarded (empty the bathwater).

Idiom works for us because of the images it gives us. Images pass information more easily and quickly than words. Think about how much information you take in instantly when you look at a photograph when compared to reading a description of the photograph. Despite the fact that idiom doesn't mean what it actually says we are easily able to use it and to understand its meaning. This is because it relates to our knowledge and experience. We can, for example, probably all remember an occasion where we have literally bitten off more than we can chew, and the discomfort, not to mention the coughing and choking that can follow.

The phrase 'thrown the baby out with the bathwater' contains two metaphors, 'baby' and 'bathwater'. Metaphors are embedded in our language. We use them without a second thought. This gives us the opportunity to enliven what we say and write. Indeed, we are so familiar with metaphors that we often understand their meaning implicitly without any real awareness they are there at all.

TRY THIS

Here are five sentences about time. Each of the sentences alludes to a metaphor, the same metaphor for all five sentences. This metaphor is not stated, yet you will understand its meaning implicitly even though you may not immediately recognise it. Read through the five sentences and see if you can identify the metaphor. Note that each sentence contains a word in italics. These provide a clue to the metaphor.

57

- » **You're *wasting* my time.**
- » **I don't have the time to *give* you.**
- » **How do you *spend* your time?**
- » **I've *invested* a lot of time in her.**
- » **Is it *worth* your time?**

Did you manage to spot the metaphor? If you are still struggling, the word you are looking for is money. Metaphors are just one of the many ways we choose to use words that mean something different from what they say. Here is another example.

TRY THIS

Can you make sense of this poem?

> **In Hackney Wick there lives a lass,**
> **Whose grummets would I woggle,**
> **Her ganderparts none can surpass,**
> **Her possett makes me boggle.**
> (From the BBC Radio programme 'Round the Horn' broadcast between 1965-1968)

Did you understand what the poem is about? Of course you did, instantly. You are likely to have identified this as an example of innuendo, a veiled comment about someone or something. Innuendo is usually humorous, a little rude and often with a sexual slant. It is a clever way of manipulating language so that we can enjoy talking about these topics without offending. We usually use innuendo just for the sheer fun of doing so.

There are some topics, when spoken about directly, can make us feel uncomfortable. Examples include bodily functions, sex and death. We have an intriguing way of getting around this problem. Let us say that you are on a coach trip and the tour guide tells you that the coach will make a comfort or rest stop. Well you know for sure that 'comfort' and 'rest' don't mean you are going to put your feet up for half an hour or take a siesta. You know this will be a toilet stop. But will it? After all, what does the word 'toilet' mean? It comes, from a French word for dressing room. Yet you know you will be engaged in an activity far removed from changing your clothes.

What this stop should really be called, of course, is a pee stop. But just a minute: it isn't a 'pee' stop but a 'P' stop we are talking about here. The 'P' is the first letter of the middle English word 'piss', from the French word 'pisse'' which in turn can be traced back to the Latin word 'pissiare' possibly from the time the Romans occupied Britain. Finally, we have arrived at the correct term: or have we?

This is an example of how we use euphemisms for politeness. There are numerous euphemisms for bathroom activities (another euphemism), sex and death, as there are indeed for murder. Here are just a few examples: 'string up, bump off, polish off, do in, knock off, top, wipe out, take out, croak, waste'.

And here is a piece of writing that you are likely to recognise. It is full of euphemisms for death from an annoyed customer returning a very dead pet parrot to the pet shop

'The parrot is no more. It has ceased to be. It's expired and gone to meet its maker. This is a late parrot. It's a stiff. Bereft of life, it rests in peace. If you hadn't nailed it to the perch, it would be pushing up the daises. It's rung down the curtain and joined the choir invisible. This is an ex-parrot.'

(From Monty Python's Flying Circus)

In times past a euphemism was a handy way to avoid profanity. For example, 'gosh' and 'gum' could be used to replace God, 'heck' to replace hell and 'darn' to replace damn. Now you can find euphemisms appearing in official language, where those in charge are reluctant to give us the bad news as plain facts. Here are a couple of examples:

» **negative patient care outcome** (the patients who died)
» **collateral damage** (the civilians who were killed)

Sometimes we choose to use words that don't just mean something different from what they actually say but completely contradict each other. Here are some examples.

- » **Found missing**
- » **Act naturally**
- » **Clearly confused**

These contradictory phrases go by the rather splendid name of 'oxymorons'. The word itself is an oxymoron; oxy meaning sharp and moron meaning dull.

Many of us enjoy using language that exaggerates; hyperbole to give it its proper name. Ordinary words such as 'nice' and 'like' are set aside as being too boring. Events and people are now labelled with the ubiquitous 'amazing' and 'fantastic'. Even the professionals get in on this act. Weather forecasts, for example, may mention, not showers but 'cloudbursts', or not high winds, but the 'threat of tornados'. Journalists may refer to a 'landmark' or an 'exclusive' rather than just an interview. (Susie Dent: The 'i' newspaper, 17/7/18)

The examples you have been reading about here have been described as a set of rhetorical devices. The set includes metaphors, similes, irony, pun, euphemisms, innuendo, hyperbole and many more. They go under the rather dull and dreary title of 'Figures of Speech'. These devices make our language appealing, exciting, and unpredictable. They well deserve a round of applause and a title that more fittingly describes the valuable contribution they make to the pleasure we take in our language.

PLAYING WITH WORDS:
PARODY, SATIRE, SLANG AND SWEARING

We are verbal artisans. We manipulate language at our whim and fancy and we play around with English just for the sheer pleasure of doing so. Here is an amusing story to illustrate.

An Indian chief decided to give each of his three squaws a brand new hide to sleep on. He gave the first squaw a bear hide, the second squaw a wildebeest hide and

the third squaw a hippopotamus hide. Within a year all three squaws had given birth. The squaw who had slept on the bear hide had a son as did the squaw who had slept on the wildebeest hide. But the squaw who had slept on the hippopotamus hide had twin sons. When the chief was asked why his squaw who had slept on the hippopotamus hide had twin sons whilst the other two only had one son each he replied, 'Oh that's easy. Don't you know? The sons of the squaw on the hippopotamus hide are equal to the sons of the squaws on the other two hides'.

(Original source unknown)

You probably worked out pretty quickly that this story is a play on the words of the famous Pythagoras theorem, taught to us in school and which states that: 'the square of the hypotenuse is equal to the sum of the squares of the other two sides'.

Here is another example of how we have fun with language.

Some girls like to buy new shoes
And others like driving trucks and wearing tattoos
There's only one thing that they all like a bunch
Oh, girls just want to have lunch
I know how to keep a woman satisfied
When I whip out my diner's card their eyes get so wide
They're always in the mood for something to munch
Oh, girls just want to have lunch

Did you pick up that this is an example of a send up, a spoof or parody, mimicking something or someone else, just for the fun of it? It's an excerpt from Weird Al's song 'Girls Just Want to Have Lunch' a parody of 'Girls Just Want to Have Fun' by Cyndi Lauper.

Parody isn't the only tool we have to give our speaking and writing sparkle. Think about satire. Satire uses humour and irony to highlight topical issues and to ridicule, expose and criticise stupidity or vice, especially in politics. Here are two examples; the first highlights a topical issue of the time and the second exposes political folly.

> **'It is a truth universally acknowledged that a single man in possession of a good fortune must be in want of a wife.'**

This opening sentence from Jane Austin's novel Pride and Prejudice, is a satire on the marriage arrangements at the time that Jane Austin was writing; women needed to marry well by marrying into money. The irony here is that it wasn't the 'single man in possession of a good fortune' who was in want of a wife but the Bennet sisters who desperately needed to find a wealthy husband because the family estate was entailed.

> **'...there have been two struggling Parties in this Empire, under the Names of Tramecksan and Slamecksan from the high and low Heels on their shoes by which they distinguish themselves.'**

This except is from Gulliver's Travels by Jonathan Swift. The Kingdom of Lilliput is dominated by two parties, the Tramecksans and the Slamecksans, identified by the size of the heels on their boots. These two parties are a parody of the two rival political parties the Whigs and the Tories that dominated the English political scene at the time that Swift was writing.

TRY THIS

What do these two pieces of writing have in common?

> **'Sblook, you starveling, you elfskin, you dried neat's tongue, you bull's pizzle, you stockfish! O, for breath to utter what is like thee! You tailor's yard, you sheath, you bowcase, you vile standing tuck.'**
> (Extracts from Falstaff – Henry IV Part I William Shakespeare)

Party people
Party people
Can y'all get funky?
Soul Sonic Force, can y'all get funky?
The Zulu Nation, can y'all get funky?
Yeah, just hit me
Just taste the funk and hit me
Just get on down and hit me
Bambaataa's jus' getting so funky, now hit me
Yeah, just hit me

(Afrika Bambaataa & Soulsonic Force: Plant Rock)

These are both examples of slang and they are around 400 years apart. Slang has been with us for a long time. We know for certain that it is as old as ancient Greek theatre but it's likely to have been in use for far longer.

Try this

Here are some more examples of slang. What do they mean? They were popular during the 1970's with one specific group of people.

- » **Grandma lane**
- » **Mobile mattress**
- » **Motion lotion**
- » **Eyeballs**

These are examples of the slang used by American truckers for sending routine messages and popularised in the film 'Convoy' released in 1978. They refer to: the slow lane, a caravan, fuel, and headlights.

Slang is often used to mark group identity and to exclude others from the group. Groups vary tremendously. They can be small and insular such as in the above example or vast, global even and loosely connected. For example, football supporters might use a slang phrase such as 'big game player' to describe a temperamental player who only scores when it counts.

Younger generations in particular enjoy taking up new words, often as a means of gate-keeping. These words are then passed on via social media until almost every young person from one end of the country to the other and further afield is using them. One example from the 2017-19 period is the slang word 'like'. This word hijacked endless utterances from the mouths of the under twenty-fives, inserted not just once in a sentence, but endlessly.

Slang quickly becomes outdated, usually as soon as it becomes popular. One sure fire way for specific slang words to become obsolete is when they are taken up by older generations. Examples of outdated slang include 'wet rag' to describe a miserable person, 'dig it' to mean to understand and 'fab' to mean wonderful: these were all popular slang during the 1950-70 period. And here are some examples of more recent, authentic teen slang. Teachers are known as 'the feds' and friends are 'squads'. Things can be 'peak' (bad), 'bare peak' (really bad) or 'dead' (really, really bad). (Charlotte Edwards: Evening Standard 18/12/18)

Language comes in handy to vent our frustrations and irritations with our job, our nearest and dearest or the world in general. Utter a good swear word or two and we usually feel much better. This handy function shouldn't be too surprising when you consider how versatile swear words are. Take the famous 'F' word; you can use it as a noun, an adjective, a verb or any way you wish.

The words we might use to swear may not necessarily start out as rude or insulting. They can be words that were in general use but which then become offensive. Take that 'F' word again as an example. Its origins are obscure but it is likely at one time to have meant 'to strike or hit'.

English, like all languages, is never static: its changes reflect the social and economic changes in society: it would be rare now to hear the words 'typing' or 'blackboard' as they are no longer relevant or appropriate for our lifestyle. At the same time new words and phrases appear, are taken up initially by a few and then by the masses. With each generation there is a desire to embrace new words thus ensuring a constant repository for our changing needs.

WHERE ARE WE NOW?

» The English language contains numerous synonyms: they provide verbal and written flexibility and choice. New words are constantly being added: some have been created to accommodate changes in society and technology whilst others have been imported from other languages.

» English is littered with words and phrases that mean something different from what they actually say: known under the broad headings of 'Idiom' and 'Figures of Speech' they give our language its sparkle.

» We are easily able to manipulate language, employing slang, satire, irony, parody and so on for our own satisfaction and pleasure.

We are immensely fortunate that English has so many words to its credit: it means we can dip into it and pull from it words of our choosing, to use, to manipulate and to enjoy. We have refashioned it and refined it to suit us. English has a history of change but it seems in the future likely to change more rapidly than it ever has in the past. Yet despite this rapid change it presents us with few problems and is unlikely to do so in the future. This is because language doesn't rule us. It never has done. Its job has always been to serve us, to accommodate our needs and if our needs change then our language must change; and it does, constantly. It will continue to be unpredictable and unruly; nevertheless, we are certainly more than up to the task of decoding it. This is the topic of the next chapter.

A selection of synonyms for the word drunk:

befuddled bent blasted blotto boiled canned dipso floating hammered happy high hooched juiced legless loaded looped mellow merry pasted pickled pie-eyed pissed plastered slammed sloshed smashed sizzled stewed tanked tight tipsy wallpapered wasted woozy zonked.

6

BREAKING THE CODE:
HOW WE MAKE SENSE OF ENGLISH

You may remember Ronnie Barker's masterly touch with the malapropism, delighting us all with his numerous mispronunciations, referring to politicians as 'pidliaticians' and newsreaders as 'nose bleeders'. We found his deliberate mispronunciations hilarious but an unwitting slip of the tongue can happen to any of us. Have you ever mistakenly said 'hung' when what you really meant to say was 'hanged' or 'affect' when what you meant was 'effect' or even 'photographic' when the word you thought you were saying was 'photogenic'? My own embarrassing unwitting slip occurred when I meant to say 'the emancipation of women' but unwittingly replaced 'emancipation' with the word 'emaciation'.

Gaffes like these are easy to understand; we are constantly working with a language that is vast, flexible and unruly. Yet we are still easily able understand each other for the simple reason that we are clever. In fact, we are language experts. We have a phenomenal ability to interpret language in whatever form it is presented to us and to use it with expertise. Perhaps this shouldn't be too surprising when you consider how long we have been speaking to each other, at least 100,000 years and probably far longer, so we've had a fair amount of time to practice.

Another reason why we are able to manage spoken language so easily comes from the help that it receives from its personal assistant, body language. As you saw in previous chapters, body language is an excellent support system for our spoken words. When we are deprived of a part of this support if, for example, someone is talking to us on the telephone, we need to listen just a little harder. And when we speak we may still move our hands and arms around even though our listener cannot see us.

We have at our disposal a phenomenal language, a language that is sumptuous, extravagant and infinitely flexible. Yet, it is also formidable, often ambiguous, nuanced, deviant and littered with quirks and anomalies. Using language is a complex and highly skilled activity because English, like other languages, is in the form of a code. It's hardly surprising that somewhere between 50-80% of our brain power is concerned in some way with language. This chapter will explore how we unravel that language code and indeed do much more. It begins by looking at how we recognise and deal with language symbols, then considers some of the ways we are able to create meaning from them. It finishes by highlighting and then challenging a few of the established rules of English.

SYMBOLS AND CODES

When we speak and when we write, we use symbols to represent our thoughts. Taken together these symbols form a code. When we speak, the symbols are in the form of sounds (phonemes) joined together to form words, phrases and sentences. When we write we are still working with symbols that are based on sound but here we have something visual on the page. We have to learn how to work out the meaning of the sound symbols we hear and those images we see on the page; in other words we must break the language code.

The first time we learn to break the language code is when we are very young. As babies we listen to the sound of the spoken words of those around us and, over time, we are able to decode their meaning sufficiently to understand what is being said to us and then gradually to begin to use these words ourselves. No one teaches us this decoding skill; we are all self-taught language decoders and we make it look effortless. A year or two later we need to repeat the whole process of decoding when we must learn to decipher those written symbols in front of our eyes so that we can read them and write them down.

Now you might think that once we have learned to speak and then to read and write, that is the end of this story; no more learning to decode language. But you would be wrong; our need to decode is ongoing. We are constantly decoding language, making sense of it, creating meaning from it and manipulating it as only real experts can do. To see how we go about this decoding business we'll look first at a language that is in the form of a very simple code.

TRY THIS

Can you decode these three language symbols: each stands for a single word?

These three symbols represent 'snake', 'walk' and 'bread'. They are in the form of pictograms, in this instance Egyptian hieroglyphics. This is unlikely to be a language you have learned to decode yet the chances are you will have been able to correctly interpret at least one and probably two of these symbols. This is because the written language symbols themselves gave you strong clues as to their meaning. Three thousand years ago all languages used some form of pictograms. Some contemporary languages still use pictograms including the languages of Japan and China. Now take a look at our own language.

TRY THIS

Here are three symbols from the English language. Taken together, they form a word we all know. Have a good look at these three symbols. Do you notice a difference between these three symbols and the symbols you've just looked at?

CAT

The difference, of course, is that these three symbols provide you with no clues to help you to work out the meaning of the word. They are just three squiggles. But you can read (decode language) so you know that these three squiggles mean a small furry animal that purrs. The point here is that, unlike those pictogram-based languages, in our English language there is no actual or real connection between the symbols and what they represent. The symbols are arbitrary, an invented pairing of three squiggles with a specific meaning. This is the case whether we are hearing the spoken sound symbols or reading the written symbols. In other words, those three symbols only mean a small furry animal that purrs because we have all agreed they should. Now this might seem obvious but this isn't necessarily always the case.

TRY THIS

Here is another written symbol, but how might you decode it? What are its possibilities of meaning? Normally you would have a context to help, such as the situation, where you are, who you are with and so on. But for the moment you are completely on your own so you will need to be creative.

X

So, what did you decide? Here are some possibilities. It could be:

1. A kiss at the end of an email from a friend
2. A multiply sign in an arithmetic book
3. A cross against a wrong answer at the local quiz
4. A notice that bars you from entering
5. A symbol to mark a spot on a map
6. A vote being cast
7. Something else

The point here is that it is you who will have decided what this symbol might mean. This is what we do with language whether it is spoken or written (and indeed with everything we experience). We are not passive, soaking up words as they are presented to us. We are active in creating meaning from them, a meaning that is significant and relevant to us. The context aids our creative efforts. You might, for example, be in a voting booth or you will have the email from your friend in front of you. But, ultimately, we decide what words mean to us. So how do we decide?

You could say that each of us has our own mental map of how the world is. Our map directs each of us to view the world through our own unique pair of spectacles.

The best way to think of these spectacles is to imagine that each pair has lenses with a slightly different tint so that even though we are all looking at the same thing each pair of spectacles will give a slightly different view. It is these spectacles that guide us in creating meaning from language.

TRY THIS

What do these three words mean to you? Would you say that they are connected in a specific way?

high speed trip

You might decode these three words as a reference to rapid journey. On the other hand, you might decode them as a reference to drugs. It is your experience that provides you with the information to make your choice. The words are the same but the decoding is different. This is how we decode and create meaning from language; meaning is personal and it depends on the knowledge and experience each of us has.

VERBAL ARTISANS

There is more at play here, much more, over and above decoding and creating meaning from language

TRY THIS

Read the following notice that you might perhaps find when visiting some gardens.

**PLEASE
KEEP OFF THE
THE GRASS**

Did you spot anything odd about the notice? Did you spot the repetition of the word 'the'?

When we create meaning from what we see or hear, we do so in a way that must make sense to us. If it fails to make sense we can even force it to do so as you might have done with the 'Please keep off the grass' notice. Well done if you saw the repetition of the word 'the' immediately, but give yourself a pat on the back if you didn't. The notice didn't make sense with the repetition of the word 'the' so your brain forced it to make sense by removing one of them. So strong is this need we have for sense and meaning that some of us are unable to spot repetition even when it is pointed out to us.

We are extremely agile in turning language that doesn't make sense into a form that does. Not only do we remove something senseless that shouldn't be there, we add things in that are not actually there and change things around until they do make sense. Here are two examples.

TRY THIS

1. Read through the following sentence.

You cn rd ths txt wtht vwls.

Did you have any problem reading the sentence as: 'You can read this text without vowels'? I doubt it as most people manage this easily. In this example you added the missing vowels.

2. Read through the following sentence.

Why deosn't the oredr of the ltteers in tihs qeustoin mttaer?

You probably easily managed to read this sentence as: 'Why doesn't the order of the letters in this question matter?' If something is in the wrong order we simply change it around so it makes sense to us.

How smart are we at juggling language? Pretty smart it seems. We can take a group of words (a phrase or sentence) and juggle it around in our heads. We can toss it up to create one meaning from it, toss it up again and it comes down with a different meaning. So agile are we at this juggling that we can do it almost instantaneously.

Here are three examples for you to play around with
- » **Stolen painting found by tree**
- » **Many antiques at senior citizen's sale**
- » **Stiff opposition expected to graveyard plan**

Earlier in the chapter you saw that there is no connection between the symbols we use and what these symbols represent, for example the three symbols that form the word 'cat'. The three squiggles only mean a small purring animal with soft fur because we have agreed they should. And this is the case with just about all of our language. Yet there is one exception to this rule. There is one small group of words where there is a connection between the words and what they mean, but the connection only exists when the words are spoken aloud, not when they are written. A small group of words has the same sound and meaning when spoken. This group of words goes under the rather splendid title of onomatopoeia. Some examples are: 'achoo', 'moo' and 'hiss'.

RULES, CUSTOMS AND FADS

It is the nature of the English language that it provides us with a more than adequate supply of opportunities to tax our brains. Yet, almost unbelievably, we have tagged onto it a plethora of rules covering English grammar, spelling and punctuation. Now you might think that these rules should assist and guide us, yet they often don't. They are complex and confusing, illogical and inconsistent. In truth they are sometimes more of a hindrance than help and just as likely to trip us up as aid us.

That being the case you will notice only scant reference here to 'good' or 'correct' English. Additionally, you'll read little more than the barest minimum about spelling and punctuation. If you are interested in semantics or you are a linguist or an English specialist I hope you will not be too disappointed. What you will read about is how competent or not our language is at its job, how well or poorly it works for us and how skilled we are at using it.

Grammar, or correct English, to give it another title, is not and never has been a set of English language rules to which we must, on pain of death adhere. Rather it is a set of customs in English usage. Many of these rules and customs are not definitive directives or edicts commanded by an English Language Police Force but an unfortunate product of fashion, introduced at various periods, often at the hand of whim and fancy. Indeed, a number of these so-called rules of grammar have been no more than passing fads. Some of them are ugly, awkward and clumsy. Others don't even make sense and there is much to be said for disregarding any that we don't like.

One good example of rejecting a clumsy rule is the one provided by Winston Churchill. This particular rule states that prepositions should not be used at the end of a sentence; yet attempting to stick to this rule can sometimes require considerable linguistic dexterity. Churchill made this point after an aide had rearranged one of his sentences by removing the preposition from the end of the sentence and placing it within the sentence. Churchill responded with the following: 'This is the sort of English up with which I will not put'. Have another look at the first sentence of the previous paragraph to see this in action.

Even trying to follow the patterns of English grammar is fraught with problems. Have a look at the following grammar pattern illustrating present and past tense:

'sink' becomes 'sank'
'drink' becomes 'drank'
'blink' becomes 'blank'
'wink' becomes ...

And this might get you into trouble.

Now take the double negative rule. This rule states that it is ungrammatical to say, 'I can't get no help today'. Grammar rules say that because 'can't' and 'no' are both negative one will cancel the other, leaving you with a sentence that means 'I can get help today'. The correct statement according to the rule is 'I can't get any help today'. Yet, as improbable as it may sound, in Chaucer's Middle English the double negative was the correct version.

Another example of so-called English misuse is when we turn a noun into a verb. Take for example, the noun 'impact'. 'The speaker made a great impact on the audience'. You will likely have come across this noun (and many other nouns) used as a verb, as in the following example; 'Overeating will impact on your health'. Changing nouns to verbs is deplored by those determined to stick to the rules of

English, yet this tradition has been part and parcel of English grammar for hundreds of years. Indeed, there is something to be said for changing any nouns you feel like into verbs. One interesting way you might consider doing this would be to use the 'ise' suffix pretty much as you might use it to change the noun 'item' into the verb 'itemise'. My own particular favourite would be the verb 'diarise' – to put into your diary.

Most of us have probably forgotten the theory behind many of these customs, those tedious English grammar lessons that we were burdened with at school. Nevertheless, we know through gut feeling when something deviates from what feels right. We may feel a little uncomfortable when we note that a grammar rule has been violated, a spelling error perhaps, or a misuse of the apostrophe. And the pedants amongst us are likely to get very hot under the collar when their eyes alight on a misdemeanour. Yet the rules of grammar, just like language itself, have always fluctuated; some rules fall by the wayside whilst new rules make an appearance. Most importantly, language exists to accommodate our needs, not the other way around. And you may have noticed that this is the second sentence in this paragraph that begins with the word 'and', another violation of a grammar rule.

TRY THIS

Each of the following sentences is grammatically wrong in some way. Read through them, see which of them, if any, feels wrong to you and make a mental note of why it feels wrong.

- » **An extensive range of lipsticks are on offer today.**
- » **When a masseur becomes qualified they can open a salon.**
- » **There are less people here today than yesterday.**
- » **When the dog trod on the mouse it fled in terror.**
- » **Writing the introduction last, making sure it covers all the points.**
- » **He was the happiest of the two brothers.**

Here are the grammatically correct sentences with an explanation of why each of the original sentences was incorrect.

An extensive range of lipsticks is on offer today.
The subject 'range' is singular and the grammar rule says the verb must agree so 'are' needs to be replaced by 'is'.

When a masseur becomes qualified he can open a salon.
The subject 'masseur' is masculine and the grammar rule decrees that the pronoun 'he' must agree. This is a good example of a grammar rule that is clumsy in practice, in this case because we don't know the sex of the subject. It makes far more sense to use the pronoun 'they' and this practice has become more accepted. This is an example of how the rules of grammar change.

There are fewer people here today than yesterday.
The grammar rule commands that 'fewer' should be used with objects that can be counted one-by-one and that 'less' should be used with qualities or quantities that cannot be individually counted.

The mouse fled in terror when the dog trod on it.
As the sentence stood it wasn't clear whether it was the mouse or the dog that fled in terror.

I am writing the introduction last, making sure it covers all the points.
This sentence wasn't complete. As it stood it didn't tell us who was doing the writing. (Grammar rules say that a sentence must contain a subject)

He was the happier of the two brothers.
The grammar rule states that 'happiest' should only be used when talking or writing about more than two people.

The important point here is to make sure that we can understand what is being said. Provided you can understand and be understood and you are able to ignore the chattering of the English Language Police Force, you may want to ditch some of these rules of grammar. In fact, almost every one of us is able to automatically think and speak grammatically. We all recognise, for example, the patterns in grammar. It is almost an instinctive exercise for us to verbally follow the rules of conjugation, that is to decide when to use, for example, 'am' or 'is' or 'are', and to settle on the correct tense for our purposes, for example when to use 'has been', 'have been' or 'had been'.

The grammar scene is certainly no rosier when it comes to decoding spelling rules. Our roller coaster language history means it is hardly surprising that we have very few spelling rules based on common sense. Another reason for this bizarre situation is that historically we have been rather lax about any sort of spelling standardisation. As new words have been introduced to the English language from other cultures we have not bothered too much about changing their spelling. When printing was first introduced, books could be printed at the whim of the printer. English spelling during this early period of printing was so arbitrary that a dictionary published in 1604, 'A table alphabetical of hard words', spelled 'words' two different ways on the title page. Even William Shakespeare was apt to spell his name as the mood took him.

TRY THIS

If you enjoy testing your skills at spelling see if you can identify the incorrectly spelt words in this list of twenty words. Check your answers with the aid of a dictionary

accommodation	liason	rythm	relavent
necessary	arguement	innoculate	business
changeable	discrete	concensus	drunkenness
harassment	independant	fourty	mischevious
embarassment	desparate	suceed	twelth

Or you may prefer to miss out on the spelling test and instead enjoy this tongue in cheek poem illustrating the dangers of relying on spellcheck.

Eye have a spelling chequer, It came with my pea sea, It plane lee marques four my revue, Miss steaks aye can knot sea.

Eye ran this poem threw it, I'm shore your glad two no, It's vary polished in it's weigh, My checker tolled me sew.

A checker is a bless sing, It freeze yew lodes of thyme, It helps me right awl stiles two reed, And aides me when eye rime.

Butt now bee cause my spelling, Is checked with such grate flare, There are know faults with in my cite, Of nun eye am a wear.

To rite with care is quite a feet, Of witch won should bee proud. And wee mussed dew the best wee can, Sew flaws are knot aloud.

So ewe can sea why aye dew prays, Such soft wear four pea seas, And why eye brake in two avers, Buy righting want too pleas.

(Source unknown)

So, what is to be said about that other grammatical irritation, punctuation? The writer and broadcaster Lynne Truss is a firm believer in the importance of punctuation and has written a book, 'Eats Shoots & Leaves' on the topic. She does have a point. Where we choose to place our commas, full stops, question marks, explanation marks, semi-colons, colons, dashes, hyphens, brackets and apostrophes will determine meaning. Have a look at the following examples, two letters with identical words but different punctuation.

Dear Jack,
I want a man who knows what love is all about. You are generous, kind, thoughtful. People who are not like you admit to being useless and inferior. You have ruined me for other men. I yearn for you. I have no feelings whatsoever when we're apart. I can be forever happy – will you let me be yours?
Jill

Dear Jack,
I want a man who knows what love is. All about you are generous, kind, thoughtful people, who are not like you. Admit to being useless and inferior. You have ruined me. For other men I yearn! For you I have no feelings whatsoever. When we're apart I can be forever happy. Will you let me be?
Yours,

Jill

(Truss, 2003, pages 9-10)

Yet we shouldn't get too bogged down with punctuation rules or indeed, get on our high horse when we encounter an infringement of a punctuation rule as long as the meaning is clear. The downfall for some of us is the dreaded apostrophe. It has a long and well-deserved reputation for bringing considerable anguish to countless numbers of us. Knowing what to do with this irksome mite is almost like being a member of an exclusive club. You are either in or you are out. If you are in you can snigger at apostrophe misdeeds. If you are out, you live in 'apostrophic' (my word) fear. So maligned and abused is the apostrophe, it even had its own protection society.

Be that as it may, the apostrophe doesn't really deserve such an elevated grammatical position as it has a pretty shaky pedigree. Whilst the apostrophe that we use to abbreviate a word, for example 'do not' into 'don't' was fairly well accepted when it was first introduced in the 16th century this was certainly not the case when it came to the introduction of the possessive apostrophe which appeared soon after. This is the apostrophe that we use to show that something belongs to something or someone else, for example, 'the dog's bone' (the bone that belongs to the dog). When this apostrophe was first introduced it was viewed with horror, being seen as ungrammatical. It was fiercely resisted and took over 100 years to achieve full acceptance.

Where are we now?

This chapter has explored the way we are able to understand the English language. It has looked at and challenged some of its rules of grammar, spelling and punctuation.

» We have a language that presents us with a number of obstacles to surmount. We need to learn to decode it as infants and then to continue decoding it throughout our lives.

» Decoding language is not necessarily about toeing the line: to a large extent we are the ones running this show. We create our own meaning from it, meaning that makes sense to us. And if something doesn't make sense we are pretty skilled at forcing it to make sense.

» We are certainly not helped in the task of decoding language by some of the grammar, spelling and punctuation rules and customs, a number of which do a poor job and may deserve to be jettisoned. We should not get too hot under the collar when we come upon a violation of a grammar rule provided we can understand and be understood.

Despite the oddities and idiosyncrasies inherent in our language, and the irritations of some of its clumsier rules, on the whole language does a pretty good job as a vehicle for us to communicate with each other. We have been using language for over a hundred millennia but how did it occur? Why did we humans first begin to speak to each other and how did it happen? Finding some answers to these questions is the theme of the next chapter.

7

THE CHATTERING SPECIES:
HOW WE FIRST LEARNED TO SPEAK

When I was a small child I loved to talk. I talked a lot, often non-stop. One day when I was around four or five years old my parents became so exasperated at my constant chatter they told me that if I didn't stop talking I would soon run out of words. I was horrified. How soon was soon? How long did I have before my quota of words was used up? How many weeks or days? Would I have any words left for my birthday party in two day's time? All these years later, much older and hopefully a little wiser I am still horrified at the thought of running out of words.

Imagine for a moment living in a world without words. What would it be like? We wouldn't be able to speak to each other, to connect verbally to anyone in order to share knowledge, wisdom, opinions, feelings and much more. Would we have a record of the things we have learned, a record of our stories and myths, both public and personal? Yes, probably, we'd have a pictorial record. Yet it would be a very different world, one without poetry, story books and plays as we know them, without letters, emails, shopping lists and so on.

There are around seven billion of us in the world today; seven billion Homo sapiens. Language has allowed us to pass on practical and creative ideas, to teach and to learn, and to share the stories that bind groups together. We have multiplied and spread, occupying just about every corner of the world. We have built cities and global networks and created diverse cultures and technologies. We are an immensely successful species and it would be impossible to deny the contribution that language has made to this success. Our exceptional achievements are the fruits of our almost endless desire and capacity for co-operation and collaboration.

When we speak we are using the skills gifted to us through almost endless generations that have gone before us and we use these skills effortlessly and seamlessly. Language is a quite remarkable achievement and it has enabled us to do marvellous things. If we had never managed to communicate with each other through language it is likely that few of our successes would have followed.

Language is so much a part of us that we don't even think about how incredible it actually is. It is an infinite ability: there is no limit to the number of words, phrases and sentences a language can have. When you think about it, the fact that we have it at all is highly improbable. Yet there it is for us to use in an almost limitless variety of ways. And of course, without spoken language we would never have progressed to written language and everything that has come since. Language is a spectacular achievement. But what do we really know about its origins?

A number of experts have given us a diverse variety of explanations for why and how we have managed to acquire this amazing skill; anthropologists, linguists, psychologists, philosophers and biologists. What they can tell us for certain about its origins is very little. In fact, they give us a very simple answer to its origins: they don't know. They don't know how, or why, or even when we first began to speak to each other. At least they don't know for certain but between them, they have come up with some unexpected and fascinating possibilities and probabilities. This chapter will explore some of their ideas and in doing so try to provide answers to the following questions:

» What is language?
» How did we learn to speak?
» Where might language have begun?
» Why did we begin to speak?

WHAT IS LANGUAGE?

We know that language belongs exclusively to our species, Homo sapiens. Other species communicate but they don't use language. Many other species make sounds. Some dolphin species use a clicking sound and whales also use whistles and a variety of squeaks to communicate. Birds produce a vast and diverse range of sounds and many of them are also excellent mimics, especially parrots, who seem to be gifted in being able to 'speak' the languages they are exposed to by copying the sounds that they hear. So good are they at this skill that we even use the phrase 'to parrot' to describe this activity. Yet no bird is able to speak because no bird has an understanding of language itself. Their brains are just not developed enough: they have 'bird brains'.

Other primates, despite being skilled non-verbal communicators, also lack a speech-ready brain, a brain capable of engaging with the key elements of language. Attempts have been made to teach language skills to chimpanzees but even after lengthy periods this success has been limited. We are the only species that can both generate and understand language.

Whenever we speak we are using around half a million of our brain cells. Just saying one word, a simple 'hello', we are engaging over a hundred of our muscles; the muscles of our face, our jaw, our mouth and throat and our lungs. And as you saw in an earlier chapter when we speak we are playing music. Our music is the spoken language played on the strings (cords) within our larynx or voice box.

One question we might ask ourselves is whether it is necessary for us to actually play this music aloud in order to say we are using language. Perhaps we could just define language as a way to make our thoughts tangible: in other words as a way for us to pin down the ideas that are going around in our heads. So, for example, if you think to yourself, 'I must remember to fill the car up with petrol', or you wonder 'Is it time for coffee and cake?' then you are using language.

Yet you might prefer to dismiss this definition, to believe that language is not just about thinking the words but about communicating them, believing that words need to be passed on before they can be called language.

Some experts believe that language exists in our DNA, that our exceptional ability for language is in our genes and therefore we are born already having an understanding of it. Although he had no means by which to provide proof of this at the time, it was Charles Darwin who first gave us the clue that our ability for language may well be something inborn.

> '…man has an instinctive tendency to speak, we see in the babble of our young children: while no child has an instinctive tendency to brew, bake or write.'
>
> (Darwin C 'The Descent of Man' 1871)

The American linguist and philosopher, Noam Chomsky was the first modern writer to support Darwin's idea that language is innate. He suggested that humans possess a built-in mental capacity or blueprint to acquire language. (To find out more Google: Chomsky N 'Aspects of the Theory of Syntax'.)

There is considerable evidence in support of Chomsky's theory. Firstly, all languages appear to be similar in structure. Every spoken language in the world possesses consonants and vowels and they all rely on joining sounds together to make words. In addition, they all have a definite framework or pattern with the sounds arranged in words, phrases and sentences and with symbols and words representing objects, actions, qualities, feelings, ideas and so on. These similarities and patterns do suggest a genetic explanation. Peoples across the world also value the same aspects of language, seeing humour, rhetorical language, metaphor, poetry and storytelling as important and desirable facets of language.

Perhaps an even more compelling piece of evidence in support of Chomsky's theory is revealed when we consider the way we learn language. If we look at children and their approach to language learning we see that even in the first weeks of life babies seem to be attracted to the sound of speech above any other sound. One of the most telling aspects of this attraction is that babies appear to prefer the high-pitched sounds that adults make when they do 'baby talk' and most interesting of all is that they are drawn to the sounds of other babies even more than the sounds made by their mothers.

Then there is the almost unbelievable skill that young children have in learning to speak. They rarely get the sentence order wrong and by the time they are around three years old most children are able to manage spoken language well. This expertise is developed even though they are not 'taught' to speak. One of the most telling aspects of their expertise is their logical approach to their language learning even though language itself is far from logical. For example, they might say, 'I runned' or, 'I eated', phrases they would never have heard. It does seem that young children appear to possess an inbuilt understanding of language.

TRY THIS

How would you interpret this sentence?

The chicken was ready to eat.

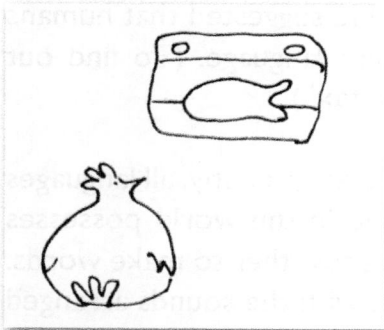

You are likely to have understood this sentence to mean that the chicken was now cooked and it was ready to be eaten. But if we take the sentence as it stands it could just as easily mean that the chicken was ready to eat its food. Yet you know this isn't the case. It seems that even very young children understand this. They appear to instinctively recognise how language works and to recognise its structures to a degree that is difficult to explain in any other way but a genetic predisposition.

Further evidence of a genetic explanation for language can be found in a recently discovered gene that might just have played a key role in the evolution of human language. This gene appears to be implicated in the role of the fine motor skills needed for speaking. When inserted into mice this gene was able to influence the control of their facial muscles, the same muscles that humans use when speaking. One other effect of the inserted gene was that it caused the mice to produce a different squeak. (To find out more Google: FOXP2 gene, MIT 2014.)

Our super-developed brains have enabled us to recognise, to create and to manipulate language in a way that no other species has been able to yet manage. But in order to do so we have needed to develop the mechanical process of speaking, a process that entails engaging our vocal cords in a way that produces coherent sounds. We have needed to learn to play that musical instrument, the larynx, and the development of this skill has been astonishing.

How did we learn to speak?

This isn't an easy question to answer because spoken language leaves us no clues to help us to work out what might have happened; no tools and no fossils. As we have so little evidence to go on it is very much a case of searching in the dark. One thing is certain; we didn't sit around one evening planning to learn to speak and then brainstorming how best to do it. All we know for sure is that at some point in our history, and probably over an extended period, we evolved from a non-speaking species into a speaking species.

We know that around five to seven million years ago humans and chimpanzees, our nearest primate relatives, diverged and we evolved into our modern Homo sapiens species. A number of the physical changes that occurred during the evolution of our modern selves since that time have been ones that have supported our transformation into a chattering species.

The first of these changes has been in the size of our human brains. We have far bigger brains than chimpanzees. Unsurprisingly, a large brain is a pre-requisite for language because language requires monumental cerebral skills. We don't really know for sure why our brains grew bigger but this wasn't the only change going on in our heads. The shape of our skull also changed; our jaw became less pronounced, the modern human jaw being significantly smaller than a chimpanzee's jaw. These changes have given us greater tongue control, an adaptation that has helped us along the road to speaking.

We have also developed longer necks. At the same time our larynx has evolved and is now placed much lower down in our neck than in other species. These two adaptations, the increase in our neck length and the lowering of the larynx, have provided us with a longer vocal tract. This has allowed us to modify the sounds we make when we speak. This adaptation also supports and enhances resonance as the sounds we make travel up the vocal tract and through the mouth.

A lower larynx has certainly been instrumental in our drive to learn to speak but it hasn't all been good news. Indeed, we have paid a huge price for this modification. It has proved to be a pretty risky development because it means that when we eat we are at an increased risk of choking. To reduce this risk we need to raise our larynx every time we swallow. Other species don't need to do this. Babies are protected from the risk of choking as their larynx doesn't begin to descend until they are around three months old and is not fully descended until about four years of age. That we have made ourselves so vulnerable to choking may give us some idea of the force of the drive propelling us towards spoken language.

Our ability to speak may have evolved alongside the development of many of our gestures. We know that chimpanzees communicate with each other using a number of gestures and so here is a possible root of many the gestures we make in our everyday interactions with each other. Indeed, as you saw in earlier chapters, gesture is just as complex as spoken language and is controlled by the same areas in the brain as spoken language.

Early on we might have copied the natural sounds that we would have heard on a day-to-day basis, such as the sound of the wind and rain or the sounds made by other animals. We may have used these sounds to name objects and actions, thoughts and possibly calculations. In 'The Descent of Man', Charles Darwin records that we might have begun to speak by copying birdsong. Birds certainly produce a vast array of diverse sounds: beep, boom, caw, chatter, cheep, chirp, chirrup, chitter, clack, cluck, crow, honk, gobble, quack, squawk, trill, tweet, twitter.

It has never been possible to prove this connection between human and bird sounds until recently; that is until we discovered more about our genes. We now know that the genes that give humans the ability to speak are the same ones that give birds the ability to sing. As the sounds we produced became more complex it is likely that we began to form distinct words. Over extended periods of time this embryonic or protolanguage would have developed structure and syntax gradually evolving into language as we know it today.

WHERE MIGHT LANGUAGE HAVE BEGUN?

We don't know for certain where spoken language originated but the African continent emerges as a strong contender. We know that this is where Homo sapiens first emerged as a species, we believe around two hundred thousand years ago although it could have been earlier. We know too that Homo sapiens began to migrate North and East out of Africa probably around 120,000 years ago, reaching the Middle East somewhere between 100,000 and 70,000 years ago and Europe around 40,000 years ago.

Possible evidence for spoken language emerging in the African continent lies in the number of distinct sounds (phonemes) that appear in a language. So, for example, the language of the San bushmen of South Africa has around 200 sounds but the further away from Africa we move, the fewer sounds we find in the languages. English, for example, has around 46 sounds and German 41. Even fewer sounds are found in languages at a greater distance from Africa. Mandarin for example, has 32 and Hawaiian, a meagre 13 sounds. (To find out more Google: 'Phonemic Diversity Supports Serial Founder Effect Model of Language Expansion from Africa'.)

It may well be that every language in the world evolved from a single 'mother tongue' that was first spoken in Africa well over a 100,000 years ago in much the same way that all humans alive today evolved from a single African maternal ancestor. It would have taken at least 100,000 years for a single language to have sufficiently diversified from that original African mother tongue to the languages further North and East. This would certainly take us back to somewhere around that time when Homo sapiens began to migrate North and East out of Africa. But we have no way of knowing for certain if this was the way it happened. It may even be the case that other, much older languages were already in use further North at the time of that migration and that those languages have since died out. Indeed, it is not beyond the realms of possibility that some form of language was used by our very early ancestors over a million years ago.

In any event, it is extremely likely that languages evolved in a similar way to how we have evolved as a species. It was Charles Darwin in 'The Descent of Man' who was able to make this significant connection between the two, suggesting that we have great diversity in languages today just as there is diversity within animal species. So, for example, when you look at wolves and domesticated dogs they appear very different even though they belong to the same 'Canis Lupis' species.

Should you care to compare the length of time we have been using spoken language to the time we have been using gestures, spoken language has a pretty short history. Even at 150,000 plus years this is just a fleeting moment when compared to the millions of years we been communicating with each other through our bodies. This may well explain why many of our gestures are unconscious, automatic and instinctive whereas, when we speak, we usually give a little thought to what we are going to say before we begin: or at least most of us do!

Why did we begin to speak?

There are a number of aspects of our human physiology and character that would have assisted us in our drive to learn to speak. For a start, our large brains provide us with an excellent storage facility; we are easily able to remember vast amounts of information, a necessary prerequisite for language. We are also exceptionally skilled at mimicking the sounds we hear. Perhaps most important of all is our human desire to communicate and engage with each other as well as our expertise in understanding other people's intentions and motives.

If we are looking for a reliable explanation that would account for why we learned to speak we are going to be disappointed yet again, because the language experts are far from unified in their theories. One thing they do seem to agree on is that necessity provided a strong impetus: we really needed to be able to speak to each other but what drove that need is in dispute. Despite this lack of agreement, these experts have provided us with some interesting theories.

Cooking

One of the most interesting ideas to emerge for why we might have learned to speak was outlined in a book in 2010 by the British primatologist and biological anthropologist Richard Wrangham (Catching Fire: How cooking made us human). Wrangham suggests that we learned to speak simply because we discovered fire and so learned to cook our food before we consumed it. The reasoning here is that eating cooked food brought us two benefits. The first was an increase in the uptake of nutrients provided by cooked food over raw food. The second came in the form of the shrinking of the gut because cooked food is easier to digest. Wrangham proposes that these two adaptations allowed the brain to grow and humans to develop into an intelligent speaking species.

Co-operation

At the heart of the theories put forward for learning to speak is our need and desire to co-operate with each other. It is generally accepted that we would have needed to pass on, among other things, the skills necessary for tool making. There is some evidence that being able to verbalise tool making skills would have been an advantage. Clearly, we are able to learn a physical skill such as tool making reasonably well by watching someone make a tool and then having a go at making it ourselves. On the other hand, if the tool-maker is able to explain what they are doing whilst they are demonstrating and we are able to ask questions, we learn more speedily and more effectively than we do if we just watch the demonstration.

Visual theft

Co-operation is also at the heart of a theory put forward by the evolutionary biologist Mark Pagel. As groups of people learnt new skills there would have been a need to protect those skills from what Pagel calls 'visual theft'. How do you stop others stealing your ideas? He suggests two options: you can retreat into small family groups or you can expand to co-operate with people from other groups. Humans, Pagel proposes, chose to expand and language was necessary to allow this to happen. (To find out more Google: Pagel M 'How language transformed humanity' TED talk.)

Gossip

Another idea that has gained increasing support is that we began to speak so that we could gossip about each other. This theory has been proposed by the American psychologist Jonathan Haidt, (The Happiness Hypothesis 2006). The gossip theory is not as daft as it might at first appear. The reasoning behind it is that within a small group, humans are able to have constant close contact with one another. They know everyone in the group; they know where each person is and what they are doing because they are close by and can be seen. They know who they can trust or not because they interact with them on a day-to-day, hour to hour basis. This close physical proximity to all members of the group was how

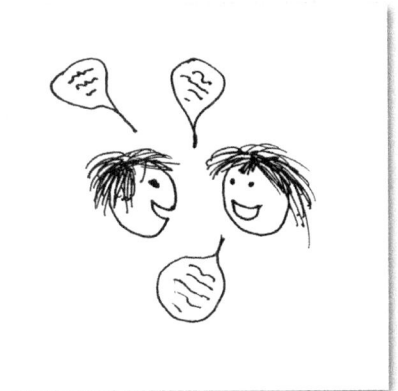

social contact and group bonding was maintained. As groups became larger it would have become increasingly difficult for members to keep in visual contact with everyone in the group. Spoken language provided a means by which all members of the group could be kept informed about each other.

Learning to speak also enabled our ancestors to tell stories. This is important; they could describe past events and they could narrate abstract stories or myths. These could be shared by the whole group and thus reinforce group identity and the all-important social bonding.

Haidt's theory is supported by the work of the political scientist Lowel Gustafson who suggests that we humans are highly social beings and it seems we cannot get enough interaction with each other. Gustafson believes that spoken language may well have developed in order to bring about this social interaction and bonding within cultural groups. In support of his theory, Gustafson reminds us that chimpanzees, our nearest relatives, maintain social bonding through grooming. Groups of chimps will sit and groom each other, picking out the dust, grit and parasites from each other's fur. Now grooming, whilst great for bonding, does have its limits, because you can only groom one chimp at a time. Once we learned to speak we were able to use spoken language to bond with a number of people at the same time. (To find out more Google: Gustafson L 'Speaking Up: The Origins of Language' TED talk.)

The gossip theory is certainly compelling. If we are tempted to dismiss it out of hand we need only to look around us and observe our fellow humans. It seems at every opportunity, on trains, on buses, in restaurants and bars we are on our mobiles, talking to colleagues, to friends, to acquaintances and to our nearest and dearest. And for some of us, if by chance we find ourselves parted from our mobiles, it would hardly be stretching the truth to say that we feel bereft.

WHERE ARE WE NOW?

This chapter has explored some of the ideas put forward by language experts about the nature of spoken language and has looked at different theories of how and why we humans might have begun to speak to each other.

> » Our species, Homo sapiens, is the only species with the ability to both understand and generate language.
> » We probably learned to speak to each other somewhere between 100,000 and 150,000 years ago or possibly even longer.
> » We may be born with an instinctive understanding of language: a genetic blueprint that enables us to embrace language learning easily.
> » It is likely that we began to speak by copying natural sounds such as bird song and that spoken language developed alongside gesture.
> » Experts are not in agreement as to why we learned to speak. Possibilities include: to co-operate with each other, to protect knowledge and skills, because we discovered fire and learned to cook or so that we could gossip.

Whether we go more for a genetic or a cultural explanation of why and how we learned to speak or believe, as many of the experts do, that both played a part, we don't really know for sure why language happened the way it did. Did we become more intelligent and so learn to speak or did language make us more intelligent?

In the next chapter we will look at the history of language itself to discover what happened once we had mastered and perfected the skills of speaking and at how we then set about changing language.

8

A MINI HISTORY:
HOW WE CHANGED LANGUAGE

A famous scene in an early Tarzan film shows Tarzan and Jane meeting for the first time. In this scene Tarzan increasingly irritates Jane by repeatedly pointing to himself and saying 'Me Tarzan' and then prodding Jane hard on her shoulder and saying 'You Jane'. This was likely to be an attempt to portray how a basic cave man language might work. It sounds feasible that our early ancestors may have spoken like this but it probably didn't happen this way. It's more likely that the first language spoken by humans, a language known as Proto-Human language, had its own set of grammar rules and the capacity to express complex ideas.

As you saw in the previous chapter, all languages in the world appear to have some similarities. So, did these different languages all develop from one language or were there already numerous Proto-Human languages in existence which then evolved into the languages we have today? We have no time machine to allow us to go back and discover how language developed so we don't know for sure what actually happened.

Whichever way you look at it you can't fail to appreciate what an incredible metamorphosis has taken place in the evolution of language, from those first early embryonic words into the complex and highly sophisticated languages of today. The story of this transformation is the theme of this chapter. It begins with a mini-history of the evolution of language and then charts the development of the English language; finally it identifies a number of current language trends.

ORIGINS

One estimate suggests that there are somewhere in the region of 7,000 spoken languages in the world today, each with its own vocabulary, structure, grammatical rules and so on. We have far fewer languages today than in previous periods of our history. Five hundred years ago there were around 15,000 languages. The trend in declining languages is forecast to continue: UNESCO predicts that half of the languages in existence today are likely to be gone by the end of this century.

When exploring the development of disparate spoken languages we are faced with a substantial problem. Speech is transient. It leaves no physical record, so there is no way a language can be identified. If we are looking for any record of spoken language, 6,000 years is just about as far back as we can go and feel pretty sure about it. This takes us to the late Stone Age when people across Europe were speaking a language known as Proto-Indo-European. (We can also talk about a Proto-Asian language and a Proto-African language.) Further back is still pretty much a mystery and we move into the realms of speculation. However, recent research by linguists indicates that European and Asian languages do appear to have a common ancestor that was in use as far back as 15,000 years ago. There may even be more ancient languages but at the moment we are unable to access them. (To find out more Google: Meade A 'Linguists Trace European Asian Languages Back to One Proto Language'.)

If the narrative of spoken language is difficult to pin down we are on safer ground with written language. We know that writing is around 5,000 years old but what came before? Surely it wouldn't have just appeared out of thin air. Research into cave paintings can give us some clues. In El Castillo Cave in Cantabria in Northern Spain, for example, a number of wall markings have been found; they are believed to be around 45,000 years old. It is thought that these markings may be symbolic. If this is the case these markings provide evidence that humans were writing much earlier than 5,000 years ago. Were these symbols brought with Homo sapiens when they first migrated north out of Africa and settled in Europe?

There is another possibility regarding the symbols in the caves in Spain. It is generally accepted that Homo sapiens migrated to Europe around 40,000 years ago. This means that Homo sapiens may not have been the species responsible for the markings. On the other hand Homo neanderthalensis was already here at that time. Could the Neanderthals have been responsible for these early symbols, or even another human species? We just don't know but it's a possibility.

One of the earliest records we have of writing now resides in the British Museum in London. It is in the form of a clay tablet, around 5,000 years old from the city of Urik in Sumar, in what was then Mesopotamia and is now Southern Iraq. This written record consists of marks pressed into a tablet of soft clay that was then left to harden. These symbols represent a record of yields of barley over a period of months.

One of the marks on this early tablet appears to represent the word Kushim. The meaning of this word is not clear but it is possible that it is the name of the person who recorded the barley yield. If so, it is likely that Mr, or even Mrs Kushim is the first person in history to have their name recorded. This early record is known as a limited script because it gives only very basic information.

Over the next thousand years writing developed concurrently in China, India and Egypt. It developed in the form of pictograms, pictures that generally represented objects. These early writings gradually evolved into what is known as a full script. A full script would include actions, ideas and so on. Egyptian hieroglyphics are an example of a full script. Over time these pictograms gradually began to look less like the objects and ideas they represented and more symbolic as you can see in the diagrams below representing a mountain.

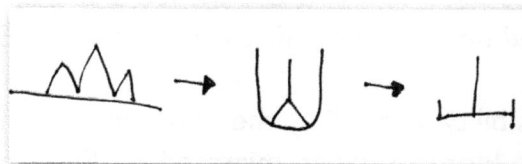

Writing continued in the form of symbolic representations of objects, actions and ideas until around 3,000 years ago. But things were about to change. A radical new approach to writing occurred at this time in the Middle East. Semitic-speaking people, Israelites, living in Egypt adapted some of the Egyptian hieroglyphics into Hebrew. In doing so they invented a system of organising symbols that vastly simplified writing. It is a system we still use today.

These new Hebrew symbols no longer represented objects, actions or ideas: each one of them now represented a sound. With this system in place you could use the same symbols joined together in different combinations to make a whole range of words. This meant you would need far fewer symbols. These Israelites had invented the first alphabet. Their early alphabet, based on consonants, had 22 symbols.

The Hebrew alphabet was adapted by the Phoenicians, people whose home was in modern day Syria and Lebanon. The Phoenicians were great traders and they spread their Phoenician alphabet across Europe.

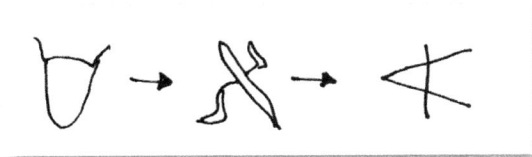

In this example above, the Egyptian hieroglyphic representing an ox (on the left) became the Hebrew aleph (an X shaped symbol). In turn this was adapted by the Phoenicians and became the letter A in the Phoenician alphabet. The Semitic/Phoenician alphabet was refined by the Greeks who added symbols to represent the vowel sounds. Over time the Greek alphabet gave rise to other alphabets including Latin on which our English alphabet is based. It seems to be the case that our own alphabet may well have its roots in ancient Egyptian hieroglyphics.

ENGLISH ARRIVES WITH THE CELTS

The Celts, also known as Britons, are the earliest inhabitants of Britain that we know anything about. The Celts were a collection of tribes, around during the Roman and pre-Roman period, that were spread across central and Western Europe from Gaul to the Iberian Peninsular and East to Northern Italy. At around the same time as written language was becoming increasingly symbolic the Celts migrated to Britain from Europe bringing with them their Celtic language, a form of Proto-Indo-European. Proto-Indo-European is the ancestor of about 400 languages and dialects including German, Greek, and Hindi. It is thought generally that the Proto-Indo-European language originated in areas of Ukraine and Russia in Eastern Europe, possibly around 5,000 years ago. There is also some support for its emergence earlier in the Anatolian region in modern day Turkey. Alas, we have no record of written Indo-European so our knowledge of it is extremely limited.

There is very little of the Celtic language left in our modern English, apart from the names of some cities and rivers. Examples are the cities of Dover and York and the Rivers Thames, Severn and Trent. The Celts themselves were eventually driven West and their language moved with them to Wales, Cornwall, the Isle of Man and Scotland. The Celtic language is still spoken today but only in scattered communities on the very Western edges of Europe, the Hebridean Islands, the coastal areas Scotland and remote areas of Ireland and Brittany.

All remained quiet on the language front in ancient Britain until the first century but the English language was about to experience the first of a number of upheavals as it embarked on a rollercoaster ride of change.

NEW WORDS ON THE BLOCK

The first of these changes came in the form of Roman legions appearing on the shores of Britain. The Romans arrived in force in the year 43CE and stayed until the early Fifth Century. The Roman influence on the English language came indirectly through Roman Latin although there aren't too many of these Roman Latin words left in use today. Some examples are Sunday and Monday, named after the sun and the moon and Saturday after Saturn the Roman god of fun and feasting. The months of the year are also a Roman legacy. January and March for example are named after Roman gods Janus and Mars. September to December relate to the Roman numbers seven to ten. Two months were added to the original ten-month year, July and August, named after Julius and Augustus Caesar.

The next major upheaval arrived from Northern Europe. From around the late fifth century until around tenth century the language of Britain came under the influence of a number of Germanic speaking peoples who crossed the North Sea and settled mainly in Eastern regions of Britain. The Jutes arrived from the Jutland Peninsular (in modern day Denmark/Germany), the Angles from the Anglia Peninsular and the Saxons from Saxony (both in modern day Northern Germany). Four of the days of the week are named after gods in Teutonic mythology: Tuesday after Tyr the

Norse god of war, Wednesday after Odin or Woden the supreme deity, Thursday after Thor the god of thunder and Friday after Frigga, who represented love and beauty. The language of Britain at this time was known as Anglo Saxon or Old English.

It was the Vikings, Norsemen and Danes from Scandinavia and Denmark, arriving in Britain in waves between the eighth and the eleventh Century, who provided the next big shake up to the English language. These newcomers were speakers of Old Norse and they left a weighty legacy, especially in East Anglia, the East Midlands and northwards to Teeside. To this day this legacy is the basis for distinct dialects between the East and West of the British Isles. Numerous towns on the Eastern side of Britain have names that end in 'by': examples include Grimsby, Whitby and Selby. 'By' is the Norse word for town or homestead. Interestingly, the word 'by' has passed into English as 'by-law' meaning the local law of the town.

Old English has had a lasting impact on our modern English. Of the 100 most common English words we use today, over 90% are Old English; these words tend to be short and express very simple ideas. Examples include, 'the', 'man' and 'have'. The Old English alphabet adopted most of the letters from the Roman Latin alphabet but was flexible and so allowed additional characters.

TRY THIS

Here is some Old English you might care to read.

Faeder ure pupe eart on heofonum, si bin nama gehalgod. tobecume bin rice. Gewurpe bin willa on eordan swa swa on heofonum.

Did you manage to decipher this extract from Old English? It is the first two lines of the Christian Lord's Prayer.

And here is an example of Old English writing.

Dan phe ðirre Olð Anzlirh Tunzan eoðe rpecan

The Norman invasion (1066) brought Norman French to England. This new language was used mainly by the ruling classes whilst the masses continued to use Old English. Nevertheless over 10,000 French words found their way into the English language, the majority of which we still use today. Common examples of Norman French can be seen in the beginnings and endings of words, prefixes such as pre-, pro- and trans- (preview, professional and transmit)) and suffixes such as -able -ent and -ance (capable, absent and abundance).

The aristocracy continued to speak Norman French and the peasantry Old English for some considerable time but gradually English returned, although French remained the language of parliament until well into 14th century. Over the next 300 years Norman French and Old English would merge to form what we call Middle English, a hybrid language that included many regional dialects. Here is the first part of the Christian Lord's Prayer again, this time in Middle English.

Oure fadir that art in heuenes halewid by thi name, thi kyngdoom come to, be thi wille don in erthe es in heuene.

And here is some writing similar to that earlier piece in Old English: this time it is in Middle English.

Than she gan to-spaken ois Middle Englysshe Tongue

How words are pronounced gradually changes over time but there is one particular change in pronunciation, occurring during the 15th century, that needs to be singled out. It was known as the Great Vowel Shift and is possibly one reason why the spelling of much of the English we use today is so inconsistent; many of our modern spelling rules are based on earlier medieval English pronunciation before the Great Vowel Shift.

Here are some examples of how words were pronounced before the vowel shift.

  » The 'aye' sound in words such as name, fame and same was originally pronounced as an 'ah' sound, as in rather and father.
  » The 'i' sound in words such as mine, fine, and time was originally pronounced as an 'ee' sound, as in bee and agree.
  » The 'oh' sound in words such as so, bow and low was originally pronounced as an 'aw' sound, as in law and saw.

Our modern English language has evolved in a rather hotchpotch fashion, a patchwork language developing alongside other European languages. You can easily spot this affinity between English and other European languages. Take the English word 'mother': it is 'mutter' in German, 'madre' in Spanish and Italian and 'matka' in Polish.

It is probably the Latin language that has had most impact on the English language, influencing it indirectly through a number of routes. The first significant influence was via the Norman invasion, the second through the Catholic church and the third during the period of the Renaissance (1500 – 1650) which brought a revival of classical scholarship, a period when over 10,000 new words entered the English language. Any number of these new words came from classical Latin and Greek, words needed to express new ideas such as 'democracy' and 'encyclopaedia'. Shakespeare himself introduced hundreds of new words into the English language including the words 'puke' (As you like It), 'bedazzled', (The Taming of the Shrew) and surprisingly, over two hundred words simply by adding the prefix 'un' to existing words; 'unsurprisingly', for example.

TRY THIS

Here are two examples of phrases you might have heard if you were around at the time of William Shakespeare. What do you think they mean? (You'll find the answers at the end of the chapter.)

» **Thou art a cutpurse**
» **I cry your mercy.**

Here is that piece of writing again; this time it is in Early Modern English.

Then she wente to spake this Early Modern Englysh Tongue

ENGLISH COMES INTO ITS OWN

The language we speak today goes under the name of Modern English. Perhaps its most striking development since the time of Early Modern English has been the speed and abundance of new words making their appearance. Colonial expansion has brought in words from far continents: 'ketchup' from China, 'bananas' from Africa and 'pyjamas', a Persian word meaning leg covering. Our Modern English has probably been influenced even more by globalisation; examples being 'latte' from Italy, 'karaoke' from Japan, 'gravadlax' from Sweden and 'fatwah' an Arabic word.

Our native language is also now less formal than in previous periods possibly because, unlike the French language, which is protected by the Academie Francaise, anyone is free to add to English as they wish. As you saw in chapter five, new words are added in a variety of ways. In truth, manipulation of existing words, much of it by journalists and advertisers, provides a constant supply of new words. We now have, for example, 'selfie' and 'ransomware'. Having absorbed the flavours from numerous far-flung places in the world we have at our disposal a rich, vibrant and dynamic language. The more we use words and the longer the time period we use them, the more they become embedded into our language.

TECHNOLOGY

It is likely that the most radical and expansive changes to Modern English are being made at this very moment as a direct result of modern technology. Take the noun 'Google'. It has metamorphosed into a verb 'To Google', understood and accepted world-wide. Another example is the word 'App' (a shortened version of the word application) a noun meaning a programme you can download to your laptop, tablet or smart phone. Numerous familiar English words have also been hijacked by technology and their meaning converted to accommodate a new situation; examples include, 'virus', 'friend' and 'surfing'.

The Internet has brought new varieties of English: these are new dialects for on-line communities. Some of these dialects have online guides on how to speak the dialect. There are even cult websites with cult dialects. One example you may care to Google is LOLCAT. This site displays some creative varieties of English, along with some rather cute looking cats.

Email alone has given us a whole new set of customs and practices that go under the name of netiquette. These practices have brought a completely new approach to communicating, one that is very different from that of letter writing. To the horror of die-hard pedants, enthusiastic emailers set about bending the long established rules of English grammar. Traditional customs of spelling, punctuation and writing style, for example the use of standard sentences with capital letters and full stops, flew out of the window, to be replaced by a quite extraordinary variation and diversity of writing style. In a way that never happened with traditional letter writing, emails can present in more or less any number of styles depending on the particular habits and whims of the emailer.

With the seemingly almost universal take up of mobile phones many of us now choose to communicate with each other via text messaging. Currently around 23 billion texts messages are sent every day. Texting, described as a cross between an email and a phone call, uses an innovative form of English that has evolved purely from technology. It has become so much a part of our modern culture that its style of communicating sometimes slips into our verbal interactions. We might even catch ourselves saying, for example, OMG (Oh my God!).

On the other hand, texting has many real advantages over other forms of communication. It is convenient for a start; most of us have our mobiles handy in our pockets or bags for whenever they are needed. Texting is also speedy; messages are usually one or two liners and simple. There are other short cuts too; we can leave out names, beginnings and endings. Texting really shows its worth to us for planning and organising both our work and our social lives. We use it for getting basic facts over, checking things out and asking questions:

- » **meeting now at 2**
- » **be home late**
- » **coffee?**

Mobile phones offer only limited screen space but this apparent obstacle has only catalysed even more creativity and innovation by trend setting texters. Non-standard characters are used alongside standard English words and characters. These are mixed and matched to suit the sender and the situation. There is a profusion of choice of non-standard characters. Here are a few examples.

- » **4 = for**
- » **121 = one to one**
- » **^^ = read message above**
- » **? = I don't understand**

Standard and non-standard characters can be joined together to make complete words and can even stand in for whole phrases.

- » **2day = today**
- » **B4 = before**
- » **XOXO = Hugs and kisses**
- » ****// = nudge nudge, wink wink**
- »

Words and phrases can also be shortened to a single letter, sometimes to their initial.

- » **Y = why**
- » **C = see**
- » **U = you**
- » **BRB = be right back**
- » **IMHO = In my humble opinion**

At other times the words might have parts removed.

- » **ZUP = What's up**
- » **SIS = sister**

Symbols can even be in the form of pictographs. The most well recognised and well used is the emoticon.

- » **(o_o) = amazed**
- » **(=_=) = bored**

Generally though, emoticons have been replaced by the newer emoji which comes in the form of a preset colourful image. Interestingly, emoticons and emojis made their debut pretty soon after texting developed. This shouldn't be too surprising as, unlike other forms of communication, with texting it is almost impossible to express the emotional content of a message. Emojis do this very important job extremely well. Another interesting comparison between texting and other forms of communication is that when reading a text message, unlike reading written language, sometimes you have to read the text aloud in order to understand what it is saying.

TRY THIS

What do these text messages say? Try saying them aloud. (Answers at the end of the chapter.)

- » **OIC**
- » **CUL8R**
- » **NAYL**

Perhaps surprisingly, texting can give us a helpful way of passing a difficult or sensitive message, one that that might be a little awkward to pass with other methods. For example, when a friend or relative is having problems you can text your concern, without any preamble, in a simple message, perhaps 'I'm thinking of you', or 'Do you need my help'? You do need to be careful to avoid confusion though; things can sometimes backfire, as shown in the following amusing illustration of a texting interaction between two people.

'im here 4 u'

'thanks – im goin thru a tuf time so it means alot…
… sorry – I lost my contacts – who is this'

'your uber driver – im here to pic u up'

Pedants have not been slow to condemn texting on the grounds that our current enthusiasm for it is sabotaging the English language. Yet there appears to be little evidence to support this view and what we see as a novel approach might not be quite as new as we think. In reality, we are already familiar with many of its characteristics. Using initials has been standard practice for some considerable time, (ASAP and NIMBY) as has the shortening of words (phone, flu and fridge). The use of symbols also has a long history (£, %, and ?), as has the mixing of the standard and non-standard (MI6, WW2).

WHAT NEXT?

If we try to look into the future of English it is almost impossible to make any solid predictions but there are some things we can be reasonably sure about. We know that the role of technology in communication will continue to expand and that artificial intelligence (AI) will play an increasingly active role. This changes things. Notwithstanding the pain imposed by grammar rules, it leaves us with questions. Will the need for any set of rules disappear? Will the English language lose some of its beauty and diversity? We just don't know.

With 7,000 spoken languages in the world today we can't fail to see that we may have a problem with global communication. This is likely to become more severe. Evolutionary biologist Mark Pagel is clear about language destiny which he believes could be a move to a world with just one language. It is looking increasingly likely that this one language will be English. There are around 400 million native English speakers in the world. This sounds a lot but it's nowhere near as many as the number of people in the world who speak English as a second language. This too changes things. The English language needs to work for them as well as for native speakers. So, the question is, what sort of English is it going to be?

WHERE ARE WE NOW?

» The history of spoken language is difficult to trace as it leaves no trail.
» We have evidence of a rudimentary recorded language that is 5,000 years old but written language may be far older. Semitic peoples living in Egypt created the first alphabet; it was spread across Europe by the Phoenicians.
» The first inhabitants of Britain that we know anything about were the Celts who migrated from Europe bringing their Indo-European language with them. Subsequently the English language has been influenced by a succession of invasions and settlements by peoples from across Europe: global trade and travel have increased the stock of English words.
» Modern English is characterised by the speed and immensity of change: technology has brought some of the most radical and rapid changes to our language.

The English language has come of age and does an excellent job for our modern communicative needs. With this in mind it is easy to assume that face-to-face communication is dominated by spoken language. This is patently not the case: as you saw in early chapters, our spoken language, our voice and our bodies work in harmony to convey our spoken messages to each other in a complex and labyrinthine process.

We have an almost limitless desire and capacity to communicate with each other. When we connect with those around us we are establishing our place amongst them, amongst our group, our human species. But what actually happens in that process, one we all engage in every time we talk to each other? This is the theme of the final part of this book.

Answers

The meaning of the two phrases in use at the time of William Shakespeare.

Thou art a cutpurse: You are a thief

I cry your mercy: I beg your pardon

The meaning of the three text messages.

OIC – Oh I see!; CUL8R – See you later; NAYL – In a while

COMMUNICATING

Chinese Whispers is a great party game. The rules are simple: one person is elected to think of a short statement, usually something amusing that they whisper into the ear of the person next to them. The message is then passed on as a whisper into the ear of each person in the line, on through however many people are participating in the game until it reaches the last person in the line.

Chinese Whispers can be a tricky game because every time the message is whispered there is a chance it will be altered. A listener may not hear the message clearly and so they pass on to the next person what they think is the correct version. By the time the message has reached the final person in the line the chances are it has been altered during the whispering stages. Now it is no longer recognisable as the original message and if it's now funnier than the original message so much the better.

There are similarities between communicating and playing a game of Chinese Whispers. Firstly, the rules for both are simple; one person thinks of a message, something they want to pass on to someone else. Secondly, just like Chinese Whispers, communicating can also be tricky because the message can get altered at any of the stages en route. Thirdly, the participants are doing the same thing, (whispering and listening or speaking and listening) but will approach the task in their own individual way. And lastly, both involve expressing emotions.

The chapters that comprise this final part of this book explore this complex process of communicating. The first chapter describes the rules of the game, how our messages to each other are passed as they make their journey from one person to another. The next chapter describes why communicating can be tricky; how and why messages can become altered at any of the stages. The following chapter looks at why, even though we are all engaged in doing the same thing, we approach communicating in very different ways. The final chapter observes our unique skill in conveying our emotions to others and offers a compelling explanation for why this is the case.

9

GETTING THE MESSAGE ACROSS:
WHAT HAPPENS WHEN WE TALK TO EACH OTHER

'D'you know what I mean?' You will recognise this throwaway phrase, one we've probably all used at some time, tossed carelessly into the conversation. Yet when we respond with a nod or a 'Yes, of course I do' we really *do* know what is meant. Why wouldn't we? Yet the ease with which we pass our ideas, our viewpoints, our emotions and much more to each other is at odds with the complexity of what we are actually doing. It also fails to highlight the sheer brilliance of our ability to do it. We are great talkers. We talk to our friends, our work mates and our nearest and dearest. We talk to acquaintances and strangers; we talk at the gym, in the supermarket queue, the coffee shop and when we are walking our dogs. We talk to give our opinion, to share our ideas and to say how we feel. We talk because we enjoy talking and because we enjoy connecting with other people.

We are a 'groupish' sort of species and talking is how we make a connection with those around us. We enjoy being with other people and we talk to them for the sheer pleasure of doing so. We talk to reinforce our relationships and to satisfy our need to feel a part of our group or tribe. We talk because, for the majority of us, the experience of not talking, if for example we were to be 'sent to Coventry' or placed in solitary confinement, the experience would be immensely painful.

We talk with scarcely a thought as to what we are actually doing; we just do it. Yet talking to each other is a complex joint project between our brains and our bodies, one that requires us to engage in monumental physical, mental and verbal dexterity. How do we manage to do this and how do we manage to almost always get it right?

This chapter will explore the complex and curious process of talking to each other, the rules of the game as it were, rules that we make appear simple and straightforward. It will look at the three stages involved, sending out a message, picking up a message and interpreting a message. You will see how the messages that we send to each other every time we talk begin their existence as thoughts in our heads, thoughts that we pass on to others through our words, our voice and our bodies. It will then look at how we listen to, and observe these messages, and finally at how we interpret and understand them.

THOUGHTS

Whenever we talk to someone else we are sharing something intimate with them; we are sharing the very contents of our mind. We pass our thoughts as a message from our brains to theirs, and to reach their brains this message needs to undertake a journey. The journey is in three stages; each stage needs to be successfully navigated before the message can continue on its journey.

So, where does the journey begin? Imagine for a moment a typical situation, any situation where you are just about to say something to someone. Consider what you might be thinking of saying to them. Your thoughts at this point are where the journey starts because all messages begin life as thoughts.

How might these thoughts appear in your head. Well, they could appear in different ways; they might be in the form of words or they might be as images. They can even appear as words and images together. Say, for example, you are thinking that you are ready for a cup of coffee and a piece of cake. Now, as you think of cake you could get a picture in your head of that very piece of cake. Alternatively you might get just the word 'cake' appearing in your thoughts. You could even think of the cake image and the word cake at the same time.

The majority of us can think both verbally and visually fairly equally but most of us tend to favour one over the other. About a quarter of us think only in words and a tiny percentage of us only in pictures. This small percentage includes the physicist Albert Einstein and the WW2 codebreaker Alan Turing. Most interestingly, even when we are thinking verbally, visual images will often intrude. This may be because our visual sense is so strong but it also suggests that visual thinking is ancient whilst language is relatively recent.

Thinking verbally is especially useful when we are dealing with abstract ideas and when we are involved in the business of analysing or interpreting. This is because language is a useful way to organise thoughts, although at the same time language does slow down our thinking processes. Unsurprisingly, we don't need language when we are thinking emotional thoughts such as those involving excitement, happiness or guilt.

Sending out a message

Let's return to those thoughts in your head appearing either as images or as words, or both. These thoughts are your intended message and the first stage they will need to navigate on their journey is to be sent out successfully. Say, for example, you're about to explain something to another person or ask them a question, or tell them how you feel and so on. Now it would be very convenient for both of you if the other person just happened to be a mind reader; they could delve into your head and have a good look at those pictures and words that are in your head. It would certainly make communicating with others more convenient but we haven't arrived there; at least not yet.

With no possibility yet of mind reading your message needs to be converted into a form where it can be passed on easily to someone else. You accomplish this by recruiting spoken words, the sound of your voice, the expression on your face and the movements of your body; this happens in synchrony and it happens instantly. Now this is some metamorphosis.

Spoken words

We can look first at those spoken words you intend to use. To make our intended words available to others our brains need to launch the mechanics of speaking. They do this by engaging the muscles of our diaphragm, vocal tract, tongue, cheeks and face. This is not all. Every time we speak, express an idea, give a viewpoint or share our feelings, we need to make a choice; it is one of labyrinthine proportions: which words are we going to use? And we have thousands of them to choose from. Our language is both vast and immensely flexible. We have evolved to produce an array of sounds that we have organised into recognisable and familiar patterns of words, phrases and so on. They can be dipped into and used as we choose in a diverse assortment of contexts. Using words to get our message across allows us to be precise because words are exact and allow us to pass a clear idea of our message. Of course, words also have the power to express the deepest emotions.

Whatever the context we are operating in we have a tremendous ability with spoken language and we make our selection without a moment's hesitation, plucking words instantly from our language memory store and manipulating them to suit our needs. We pass and receive thousands of words every day and can speak at the rate of around a hundred and fifty words a minute, constantly making endless tiny adjustments to they way we pronounce each syllable. The average British person has around 27 conversations a day lasting on average about ten minutes.

Although we express ourselves through spoken language with considerable adroitness we do it in a rather lax and fuzzy way. We think we speak using distinct words; in practice things are a little different. Spoken language doesn't flow out of our mouths as distinct words, phrases and sentences but in a continuous stream of sound with everything more or less jumbled up together. Nor do we speak words as we think we speak them.

TRY THIS

Say the following words aloud and mentally note what you are actually saying

» **parliament**
» **chocolate**
» **library**

You probably found yourself saying pahlament, choclet and liebree. These verbal short cuts allow us to get our words out faster than we would be able to if we sounded out the syllables in every word and separated our words and sentences with pauses.

Voice

Our spoken words are accompanied by the sound of our voice. We tend to think of these two as being pretty much same but as you saw in chapter three, our voice is extraordinarily adept in passing messages that are completely separate from those contained in the words we use. Our voices are constantly employed in conveying their own meaning of what we are saying through changes in intonation, pitch, pace, melody, emphasis and so on.

The backing group that we looked at earlier, comprising coughs, ums, laughs, pauses and others of that ilk, each with a particular part to play, will also have its own agenda. One example is when we deliberately pause or cough if we need time to think before speaking. Not all messages that we send via our voices are intentional. For example, in a stressful situation we may well, unintentionally and unknowingly, raise the pitch of our voice.

Whilst we are engaged in speaking, our ears stop working so we don't hear the sound of our own voice in the same way that other people hear it. We hear it through our body so it always appears lower to us than it actually is. This is one reason why our voice seems to sound different when we record it and play it back.

Body language

Whilst our spoken words and our voice are working hard in unison, our facial expression and our body will engage to proffer their own complementary language to support our words and voice to get our message across. As you saw in chapter three this supporting cast will offer intentional messages such as using a thumbs up gesture to indicate success or perform a high five as a greeting. This cast will also send unintentional messages, for example unconsciously nodding our head as we say yes or shaking it when we say no. All work together with one shared aim in mind; to send that message out so that it is easily available to be heard and seen.

Picking up a message

Having sent your message out it now needs to be successfully picked up and this is the second stage of its journey. Just as we have three ways to get our messages across to other people, when they talk to us we have three ways to pick up their messages. We listen to their spoken words, we listen to the sound of their voice and we watch their body as they speak.

LISTENING

Listening and observing is the second stage that messages need to successfully. We are skilled at listening to spoken language. Even though we are likely to hear words spoken to us jumbled together and delivered at an awesome rate, we seldom fail to understand what we are hearing. We can instantly pick up on words that belong to a specific regional or national dialect; we can recognise and interpret idiom and metaphor with ease and handle all the subtle nuances of language without hesitation.

One of the most useful skills we possess when listening to spoken language, one that really comes into its own when we are engaged in conversation, is our ability to predict. We are great predictors. This skill is just part and parcel of the normal process of communicating with each other, and it enables us to decide ahead how we are going to respond to what we hear. We predict what the other person is likely to say so that we can plan what we might say in response. We predict whilst the other person is talking to us. In fact we do it continuously and we are so skilled at it we can sometimes find ourselves predicting what they are going to say even before they have worked it out themselves. We may even be tempted to finish their sentences for them.

TRY THIS

Here are a couple of phrases: you might enjoy predicting how they finish.

All politicians are...
Italian men make excellent...

You predicted of course that all politicians are honest and that Italian men make excellent pasta!

We have a goodly ability to glean personal information from the sound of someone's voice. We can recognise whether they are male or female, we can get an idea of their age, their social and geographical background, how they are feeling and so on. We pick up on their accents and their vocabulary and then use everything we have discovered to work out some likely aspects of their personality; to perhaps decide whether they are trustworthy, dominant, attractive and so on.

Watching

We may be talented when it comes to dealing with spoken language and voices but it has to be said that when it comes to observing body language we are superb. Unlike listening to someone speak, watching them is not something we even have to think about; we do it naturally, instinctively and unconsciously. Indeed, watching someone's expression as they speak to us really does help us to understand what they are saying. We can easily tell when they are about to say something to us, we can recognise instantly whether they are feeling happy, angry, sad and so on. The reason why we are such experts is very simple; we have been engaged in this extraordinarily complex activity for a very long time.

Try this

What are the messages in this image?

You can probably see that the message Jo on the left is sending is that he is feeling a little blue, perhaps a little sad or worried. The message sent by Fred on the right is one offering support, wanting to help and trying to make things a little better. You will have easily interpreted these messages and you will have done so the instant you looked at the image. You will also have understood this scenario effortlessly even though to do so will have entailed your noting at least six separate body signals. Here are the emotions being expressed and the pertinent body signals.

1. Jo is expressing sadness and anxiety. His mouth is turned down and his head is bowed.
2. Fred's face and body are expressing concern and support. His head is tilted to the side; this gesture indicates support and friendship as its origins lie in appeasement. His touch on Jo's shoulder indicates friendship and support. His open body stance and his open hands indicate openness and friendship as they signify nothing hidden.

Individually these body signals can be interpreted in any number of ways. For example, a touch on the shoulder can be used to congratulate, a bowed head could mean shyness but it was your reading of the whole picture that told you that neither of these was the case here. This is quite an accomplishment in a split second and is what I mean when I say that we are experts.

We are almost always unaware of the massive amount of information we receive from others just by listening and watching. When you think about it, this is quite a feat, being on the receiving end of another person's message, taking in three different sources of information at one go, yet we do it effortlessly. Together these three sources of information – words, voice and body language – offer us the complete picture of the message.

INTERPRETING A MESSAGE

Having been successfully picked up, the message has now moved on to the third and final stage that it will need to navigate as it continues its journey; it will need to be interpreted. Our brains immediately get down to this task: we note what the words are saying, what the voice is saying and what the face and the body are saying. Both sides of our brain are employed to carry out this job of interpreting the messages.

We use the left, more rational side of the brain to process language. But the right, more creative side also has a vital job to do. This right side of our brain is the intuitive side, the side that picks up on all the subtleties and nuances of communication; the intonation, the humour and so on. It is also the side that processes what we see, so body language and especially facial expression will be interpreted here. And because emotions are generally expressed through body language, it is this right side of our brain that helps us to pick up on the feelings that are expressed in every interaction.

You might be tempted to think that this final stage of the journey should be plain sailing but this is certainly not the case. Interpreting what other people say to us is probably the most complex of the three stages. Interacting with others would be far easier if we were computer-generated beings but we are, in truth, highly individual human beings. This means that each of us has a slightly different take on the world.

Each of us uses our experience and our knowledge to interpret the world around us and each of us experiences everything around us, what we see, hear, feel and so on, in a unique way. As you saw in the chapters on language, we don't just passively soak up everything we receive through our senses: we create from it our own individual meanings, meanings that are filtered through our experience and our expectations. And any meaning that we create from what we see, hear, read, or indeed any information we receive through our senses must make sense to us.

When others speak to us we work hard to ensure that what they say does make sense to us. Yet the meaning that we place on their words could well be different to their intended meaning. Here is an example to illustrate. When attending a church service a small child heard the hymn, 'Gladly The Cross I'd Bear'. What meaning did she create? Why, the hymn was about a bear, called Gladly who was cross-eyed. This was the meaning that made sense to her.

We strive to make sense of someone's body language in a similar way but with one fundamental difference. Much of our interpretation and understanding of voices, expressions, gestures and so on relies on our intuition. When we say we respond to someone intuitively, that immediate, automatic feeling we can have about another person, it is usually because we have unconsciously picked up on the messages contained in their body language.

Intuition just cannot easily be explained in any way other than by gut feeling. This should hardly be surprising when we recall the ancient and instinctive origins of much of our body language. And interestingly, although we know a great deal about how our brains interpret language, and even how we make sense of some gestures, as yet we have no real understanding of how our brains 'read' body language.

Notwithstanding these differences, when we interpret body language we do exactly the same as we do when interpreting language, we create a meaning from it that makes sense to us.

TRY THIS

Look at the drawing below. What does it mean to you?

What did you see when you looked at the drawing? Was it an old man's face or an image of a woman sitting with her head on her knee? This is just a party trick image of course, a bit of fun, changing the image, seeing one interpretation and then another. Yet the point is made that it is you who is running this show; you are creating your own meaning from it.

When in conversation we interpret everything as a single scenario; words, voice and body language. We do this pretty rapidly as first impressions take only a few seconds to form. We use our experience to make a number of calculations that help us to interpret what others say. We consider who is speaking to us, what we know about them and what expectations we have of them as we take in their message. Above all, these disparate aspects do need to appear reasonable to us, they need to make sense. Making sense of what we hear and see is not a passing whim. It is vital to our wellbeing. The American anthropologist Clifford Geertz summed it up.

'The drive to make sense out of experience is as real
and pressing as the more familiar biological needs'.
(Geertz C, *American Anthropologist* 59(1):32-54)

Geertz believed that our need to make sense out of our experiences is as important to us as our need for food. So vital in fact, that if something doesn't make sense to us we create something that is different. In other words, we see what we think and expect we should be seeing and we hear what we think and expect we should be hearing.

Here is a story to illustrate just how complex and finely tuned these judgements are.

On a cold January rush hour morning, a busker began to play the violin in a metro station in Washington DC. During the 45 minutes that he was playing, a small boy stopped to listen but after a couple of minutes his mother hurried him along. Several other children did the same; few of the thousands of adults passing by had the time to stop and listen. When the busker came to the end of the six Bach pieces he was playing no one even noticed. The violin playing was part of a social experiment organised by the Washington Post. The violinist was Joshua Bell, one of the best musicians in the world and two days earlier he had played to a full theatre in Boston where the price of seats averaged $100.00.

In this story the good people of Washington DC saw and heard what they expected. They expected to see and hear a busker playing his violin to make a few dollars and this is how they interpreted the musician and the music he was playing. Their experience told them that the scene they were observing only made sense this way.

Two-way messages

So far it looks as though we send messages in one direction only but, in reality, messages are constantly being sent both ways. Even when we are listening to someone speaking to us we will be passing a host of messages back to them through our bodies; through eye contact, nods, smiles and so on. Communicating with each other is a two-way process with messages constantly crossing backwards and forwards. And this is true whether we are having an informal chat with a friend or giving a formal presentation to a massive audience.

You might think that if you were to give a formal presentation your audience would not participate at all, but even in this formal scenario this is not the case. You would receive from your audience a continuous stream of messages; these would be sent from their faces and their bodies. Hopefully, their expressions would indicate interest and enjoyment rather than puzzlement or boredom, but if by chance someone fell asleep, that would definitely be an unwelcome message to you.

WHERE ARE WE NOW?

» We make communicating with each other appear simple and effortless, yet it is complex and requires a huge amount of brainpower.
» Every time we talk to someone else we share the contents of our mind with them: every message that we send begins life as a thought; these thoughts can be in the form of words or images or both.
» All messages need to undertake and successfully navigate a three-stage journey: they are sent out, picked up and interpreted. Their journey begins with the thoughts in our heads that we wish to share with another and their destination is the meaning created by that other.

What I have set out in this chapter is basically a theoretical rather than realistic description of how we get our messages across. It would certainly be perfectly apt if we behaved just a little more like those robots I mentioned earlier. But we are very much individual human beings with all that being unique entails and that changes everything. It means that just like when we play the game of Chinese Whispers, talking to each other can be tricky.

Messages can become altered at any one of the three stages they have to navigate en route to their final destination and there is just no guarantee that any message will make it to its final destination intact, in other words identical to the original thoughts of the sender. Probability seems to indicate that this is highly unlikely to be the case. The fact that we usually do get it right, despite the potential for failure, is testament to our own quite astounding expertise and artistry in communicating with each other. This expertise is the theme of following chapter.

10

GETTING THE MEANING:
WHY TALKING CAN BE TRICKY

Is the following scenario one that is familiar to you? You are about to say something; it was there in your head, but then you lose the thread of what you were going to say. Or you begin to speak, something distracts you and everything flies out of the window. The more you struggle, the more the words that you are searching for fade away. Yet all is not lost because once you relax a little your brain decides to play ball and those irksome words are there for you. If this is something you have experienced you are far from alone. Our thoughts sometimes struggle to change themselves into words because our brain refuses to co-operate. It happens to all of us at some time or another and it is just one example of how messages can fail to get through. In this example the message didn't manage to navigate the first stage of its journey, it failed to get converted from thoughts into words.

THOUGHTS → WORDS VOICE BODY → EYES EARS → THOUGHTS

The journey that messages need to take is illustrated in the above model. You saw in the previous chapter that messages start as thoughts in one person's head and finish as thoughts in another's head. These messages can flounder at any of the three stages in the journey which are represented in the model above by the three arrows. In this chapter you will see illustrated a number of reasons why messages may flounder on their journey. It explores why our thoughts may not be spot on when they are changed into our spoken words, voice and body language. It looks at why hearing someone's words and observing their body language may not always be successful and why interpreting what we hear and see can bring its own problems. Above all, this chapter will demonstrate how and why, despite the potential for failure, messages are usually successful in reaching their destinations more or less unscathed. As you read through the examples and explanations, some of the scenarios described here may seem familiar to you. You may recognise someone you know; you may even recognise yourself.

CHANGING THOUGHTS INTO WORDS, VOICE AND BODY LANGUAGE

This first stage is a complex one for our messages to navigate. One common problem they may face at this stage occurs when our spoken words, our voice and our body signals don't work in harmony. When there is conflict between these three it's rather like they are having an argument and so our messages may become muddled. We send out these muddled messages for different reasons; sometimes deliberately but at other times unknowingly. Here are some examples. In each of them the words say one thing but the voice and the body communicate something different.

'YOU LOOK GREAT!'
In the following example the conflict between the words and the voice and body language is deliberate.

TRY THIS

It's a good idea to do this in front of a mirror. Imagine you are out shopping with a friend or perhaps with your partner and they have tried on an item of clothing. They emerge from the changing room to ask you whether the new item suits them. Let us say that their chosen item of clothing doesn't look good. Now say out loud 'Oh yes, it looks absolutely wonderful', but say it in a way that really means 'It looks dreadful'. Note what happens to your voice and your expression.

This is an example of sarcasm of course. Your words are a lie. What is the likelihood that the message will successfully navigate this stage? It's just about certain to make it. Even though your words are a lie, your voice and your body will have successfully passed the truthful message.

Sarcasm is often used for amusement but it also has a negative aspect. It can be rude, aggressive or a put down and is often delivered with considerable subtlety. Some examples include, 'Fine, whatever', 'You don't say' and 'Can't you take a joke?' On the receiving end, the aggression can be hard to spot yet we understand the put down aspect intuitively because we tune in to the body language so effortlessly. We may feel uncomfortable even though we might not necessarily recognise why we feel this way.

Sarcastic messages almost always manage to navigate this first stage. This is because not only are our bodies, and especially our voices, immensely skilled at passing them but, on the receiving end, we have considerable skill in picking up even the most nuanced aspects of communicating. One exception is when sarcasm is aimed at young children: until they are around six or seven years of age they won't have been through the social experience that helps them to understand how sarcasm works.

In the following examples there is also disparity between the words and the body language. The difference here is that rather than this being deliberate it is likely to be more unconscious and unintentional.

'I'M FINE!'
You are struggling to balance your bank statement. Try as you might the numbers just won't agree. You are tight for time and feeling frustrated. Let us say that someone, perhaps a friend or colleague or your partner asks you if you are OK and offers to help. Now it is possible that you say, 'Yes please, I'm struggling, I'm fed up and need your help'. On the other hand, because you are feeling frustrated and irritated, you might just find yourself saying 'I'm *fine!* I can manage', even though you know you are struggling. Despite your words being untrue, the message has no problem navigating this stage because your body language is doing such a splendid job.

'JUST LOOK AT THIS MESS!'
In this scenario you have just washed the kitchen floor. Within minutes someone walks in with muddy shoes, leaving messy footprints all over your clean floor. Now what message might you wish to pass? It could be how you are feeling: fed up

perhaps, frustrated, angry or disheartened. Or the message could be that you want the muddy shoes removed at the door and the culprit to wash the floor again. These thoughts and feelings are your message but instead of expressing them you hedge around them. You might say instead, 'Just look at this mess!' or perhaps 'Do you *have* to?' or 'Can't you see I've just washed that floor?' Yet despite these red herrings, your message will navigate this stage without difficulty. You will be understood loudly and clearly by anyone paying just an iota of attention to your voice and your body.

The emotions that trigger this hedging can apply to numerous irritating and annoying situations: slamming the car door, leaving the top off the toothpaste/the toilet seat up/newspapers scattered around and so on. There is a problem here though. Hedging becomes a habit, slipping easily into nagging and moaning and when that happens other people stop listening. When others stop listening it becomes pretty near impossible for messages to navigate this first stage of their journey with any realistic chance of success.

'I'LL BE OK'
The following example is similar to the two previous examples insofar as it occurs largely unintentionally. The difference here is that it is manipulative, albeit unintentionally. When you see this example in action you are observing a real skill in using language and body language to manipulate although the manipulator is unlikely to be aware that they are doing so.

You are planning to go out with a group of friends for the evening. Your plans will mean that your partner will be left to their own devices for the evening. As you say goodbye, your partner responds with, 'You go. Have a good time. I'll be OK. I think I might have a book here that I can read'. Alternatively, you are visiting your elderly father. You tell him that you won't be able to visit for a week because you will be going on holiday. Your father responds to your news with, 'I've got the TV. It's not all that great but it will fill the time'.

The message in both of these scenarios is, 'I don't want you to go. I will be miserable here on my own', but the chances are that your partner or elderly father will be unaware that they are not saying it with words. Yet their message will have no navigational problems here because it will be delivered expertly in the sad face, the sigh or the drooping shoulders. These body signals will express their feelings of anxiety or anger that lie at the heart of this message. There are numerous variations of manipulative communication; they often take place within family situations and the message almost always manages to navigate this first stage with ease.

SULKING

In this final example it is body language that says everything; the message is passed easily without any help whatsoever from words or our voice. All that is required is action, the action of severing verbal communication. You feel annoyed or upset at someone for a specific reason. And this is the message. Yet you don't speak these thoughts and feelings; instead you say nothing, but your message flows across, simply by the act of severing verbal communication.

These are just a few of the many examples that illustrate how our messages manage to navigate, almost always successfully, some of the tricky parts in the first stage in their journey en route to their final destination. Having been successful they now need to navigate the second stage of that journey. When we speak our words and our voice need to be heard and our body language needs to be observed.

HEARING AND SEEING THE MESSAGE

TRY THIS

Stop what you are doing and for one complete minute, just sit and listen to the sounds around you. Note what you hear in that minute.

You may have heard music, the sound of voices, humming machinery, a clock ticking, traffic noise, perhaps even a bird singing, a dog barking or something else. Are you surprised at the number and variety of sounds around you? There is something else you might have noticed; it is that listening requires a certain amount of concentration. The chances are that you were unaware of most of the sounds you heard until you listened for them. The point is those sounds you heard didn't just appear when you began to listen. They were there all the time, available to your ears but you just hadn't heard them.

We are pretty good at fooling ourselves into believing we are listening. We are even better at pretending we are listening, fooling the speaker that they have our undivided attention. In reality our minds are somewhere else, perhaps thinking about jobs we need to get done or focused on that glass of wine we will have later. There are a number of reasons why we don't listen; here are just a few of them.

WE ARE BOTHERED

Listening can be hard for us if we are bothered for any reason. Perhaps there is a practical reason. We have been sitting too long, the chair is hard, our legs feel numb or our back is aching. Alternatively, the room is sweltering and we are gasping for a cool drink or the opposite; the room is freezing and our teeth are chattering. All we want to do is get up and move around. Someone is speaking to us and we struggle to pay attention. Only a small amount of the message may manage to get across to us.

We might be bothered about what we are hearing because we don't agree with what is being said. It might be a point of view, perhaps a political opinion that is at odds with our own. Or someone is moaning or nagging us. We don't like to be nagged so we do our best to stop the message getting across to us.

WE ARE BORED

There are different reasons why we might be bored. Perhaps it's the subject we are listening to; it's about sport and we hate sport, or a film we've not seen and have no interest in seeing. Or perhaps it's a friend or colleague who rambles on about their job, their car, their dog, their kids or their holiday. We have heard it all before and don't wish to hear it again. When we are bored only a small portion of the message will be successful in getting across yet we are skilled enough to pick up the basics and convince the speaker that we have not only heard everything they have said but that we are interested in what they are talking about.

We are busy

We don't listen when we are busy doing something else. We might be cooking and need to concentrate on weighing out the correct quantities. Or we might be on-line engaged in some research or involved in a game. Someone, perhaps a family member, or a colleague interrupts our activity to tell us about their shopping trip, round of golf or lunchtime meeting. Our mind is on what we are doing and so we may well hear only part of the message.

We are planning

Sometimes we fail to listen because our mind is focused on planning what we are going to say in response to what we are hearing. Now planning ahead what we are going to say is a normal part of communicating. We need to do this in order to be prepared for when it is our turn to speak. But when we focus exclusively on planning what our next line is going to be, listening is forced to take a back seat and we actively stop the message from getting across.

We prefer to talk

Unsurprisingly, there are some of us who just prefer to talk; this leaves no space for listening. We have all met people who do this; we find them at work and when we are socialising. We might even have someone like this in our own family. They just don't want to listen; they only want to talk, often non-stop. Those who prefer to talk are generally poor at reading the body signals of the people around them. They don't register their lack of interest. They don't register the discomfort others are feeling. Nor do they recognise that another person wishes to speak. They are also likely to interrupt other people when they are speaking and to talk over them.

We are bogged down

Try this

Here is a question to consider. As you read these words are you aware of the feel of the seat you are sitting on? (If you are standing this will be the floor beneath your feet.)

I would wager a considerable sum that you weren't aware of the feel of that seat until the moment I brought it to your attention. There is a good reason for this; it is to avoid overloading our brains with unnecessary information. We are constantly bombarded with stimuli that we receive through our senses: sight, hearing, smell, touch and taste. If we were aware of all the sensations we receive, all of the time, our brain just wouldn't be able to manage this massive input. So when you first sat down on your seat you would have needed to be aware of its feel, but once you were safely seated this was no longer necessary and so your body ceased to be aware.

This awareness applies to all of our senses. You can probably remember an occasion where you were faced with an unpleasant pungent smell but after a short while you just got used to it and it was no longer a problem. Our sense of hearing is no different. Our brains switch our hearing off to those sounds that are not needed.

When we don't listen, or only partially listen, messages really struggle to navigate this second stage of their journey. Even body language is unable to step in and help out in many of these situations because when we fail to listen we may well fail to look. Sometimes the messages just give up the ghost and then they really have failed not only to navigate this second stage in their journey but to reach the third and final stage, the business of being interpreted and understood.

UNDERSTANDING THE MESSAGE

We cannot say that messages have reached their destination until they have successfully navigated the third stage of their journey; they have been successfully interpreted and understood. There are two players involved here, each with a key role to play in any message's chance of successfully navigating this stage. The first player is the English language and the second is our personal perspective.

THE ENGLISH LANGUAGE: IT CAN BE A LITTLE SLIPPERY

In chapter five the quirkiness and unpredictability of our language was illustrated in some detail. English certainly has the potential to put a few snags in our way; idiom, jargon, and slang to name just a few. It also presents plenty of other opportunities for message failure but we know that we are almost always more than up to the task of negotiating our way through this linguistic minefield. Here are a couple more examples of English snags that have the potential to derail our message.

The following words seem designed to confuse. They sound the same but are spelled differently and have different meanings.

Discreet: meaning showing reserve or prudence
Discrete: meaning distinct or separate

Compliment: meaning praise, congratulations or good wishes
Complement: meaning an accompaniment, addition, accessory or quota

Other English words are just so arbitrary that we are faced with an extraordinary amount of flexibility when trying to make sense of them. This has the potential to become a recipe for confusion. How do we decide which to choose?

TRY THIS

Look at this list of words and phrases; each of them indicates frequency.

» **From time to time**
» **Sometimes**
» **Frequently**
» **Occasionally**
» **Regularly**
» **Often**
» **Now and then**
» **Constantly**
» **Repeatedly**

Take a piece of paper and write the word ALWAYS at the top and the word NEVER at the bottom. Next put the words and phrases in the order you think they should go in relation to ALWAYS and NEVER.

Did you have to think carefully about where to put each word or phrase? If you were to ask someone else to do this, the chances of them putting the words in the same order as you have are pretty slim. Words that have similar meanings and which can be used in place of each other give us plenty of choice but can also create ambiguity of meaning. When your boss tells you that she needs to be updated regularly, your interpretation of regularly may be very different from hers!

PERSPECTIVE: A PAIR OF UNIQUE SPECS

Notwithstanding the difficulties that messages might have encountered so far, it is our individual perspective that poses the greatest threat to their success at navigating this final stage. As you saw in chapter six perception is rather like each of us wearing a unique pair of spectacles: each pair having lenses of a slightly differently hue. As we look out though our individual spectacles we interpret everything we experience in our own unique way. Consider what a particular smell might mean to you, perhaps one that triggers a distant memory possibly the old-fashioned perfume used by a favourite aunt. The meaning you might give to that particular smell will be a very personal one.

You saw in the previous chapter that when others speak to us we use our experience to make a number of calculations that help us to interpret what they say. We consider who it is that is speaking to us, what we know about them and what expectations we have of them as we take in their message. Above all, these disparate aspects do need to appear reasonable to us; they need to make sense.

TRY THIS

Here is an old riddle. Read through it and make a mental note of how long it takes you to work out the answer.

A man and his teenage son went mountain climbing. The son fell and sustained a serious injury. He was rushed to hospital and taken straight into theatre. However, the surgeon recognised the boy and said, 'I can't operate on him, he is my son'. How could this be?

How long did it take you to work out the answer to the riddle: five seconds perhaps, thirty seconds, or did it take longer? The point here is that unless you recognised instantly and automatically, without even needing to think about it, that the surgeon was the boy's mother, you will have heard (read) what she said and judged that a surgeon is a man not a woman. You will have made this judgement based on your own experience and expectations of what seems reasonable and what makes sense to you.

When you consider the unique nature of our spectacles you may wonder what the odds might be of any messages successfully navigating this final stage in its journey. How likely is it that we will interpret messages so that their meaning is identical to the original thoughts of the sender? It would seem highly unlikely. So, it might be more useful to say that messages have successfully reached their destination once we have created our own meaning from them, even if that meaning is different from the original thoughts of the sender. Hopefully this meaning will be close enough to the original. Despite having to navigate each of these three stages most messages get through and we mostly excel in understanding each other. We are, in truth, exceptionally adept at this task. One major explanation for this high success rate is likely to be found in our supreme ability both to exhibit and interpret the nonverbal elements of any message; these provide us with a prodigious amount of both factual and emotional information. Nevertheless, whenever there is any conflict between words and body language it is almost always the body language that passes the message and so saves the day.

WHERE ARE WE NOW?

» Our spoken words, voice and body language are sometimes in conflict rather than working in harmony.
» We may not listen if we are bothered, bored, busy, bogged down, planning or we simply prefer to talk.
» The English language can be tricky but not as tricky as the unique spectacles that dominate the way we interpret messages.
» This chapter has illustrated some of the potential opportunities for our messages to flounder. Despite these risks, most messages manage to navigate the three stages in their journey to successfully reach their final destination.

When we communicate with others we are all employed in the same activity. Yet just like when we play the game of Chinese Whispers each of us will have our own approach to this activity; we will go about it in our own individual way. This diversity of approach to communicating is the topic of the following chapter.

11

DIVERSITY IN ACTION:
HOW WE ARE THE SAME BUT DIFFERENT

Many, many years ago, as a teenager, I picked up a well-known newspaper and for the first time enjoyed the cartoon strip about Charlie Brown and his friends. I was particularly taken with one of the characters in the cartoon strip. This character was obviously a girl: I say obviously as she had the same shoulder length hair, cut in the same bob style as myself. I admired her because she was gutsy: you could tell this by her upright posture and her slight swagger when she walked. She also appeared to be exceptionally confident in speaking up and voicing her opinion. She was, for me, a totally unexpected, surprising and rewarding character and I was immensely pleased with her.

Yet somehow a part of me couldn't quite believe that I'd been lucky enough to discover such an impressive female cartoon character. Something wasn't quite right. She appeared to be just a little too much like a male cartoon character to be completely credible to me. I was right to be doubtful. Peppermint Patty was a girl created for a specific purpose, to persuade women into sport and the way her creators had decided to accomplish this was to make her behave like a boy. I was staggeringly disappointed. I should have listened to that hint of doubt; it was clearly telling me I was observing the assured and nonchalant use of language and body language that is usually portrayed in images of boys rather than girls.

Notwithstanding my own abrupt coming down to earth, when we think about variation in how people communicate with each other, differences in the way men and women communicate may not be the first thing that comes to mind. For the majority of us it is more likely to be the diversity of languages in use today and the fact people in other cultures may well use gestures that are different from ours.

Without doubt there does exist a vast cultural variation in both language and body language between people of different nations. Yet we don't need to travel this far from home before we observe a significant and diverse array of communicating styles. Indeed those nearest and dearest to us are likely to provide us with much of interest to observe. This is because, although our communicative behaviour can be described, and is illustrated in this book, as belonging in the same way to all of us, we are very much individuals. We are all the same insofar as we all use spoken language and body language to communicate yet we are also different; we do it our own way. Indeed, we are more than individual; each of us is unique and this means of course that each of us will have our own unique way of communicating.

Attempting to describe this vast array of unique communication styles would be well nigh impossible. Nevertheless, we can go some way to illustrating some of the more easily observable differences by looking at a number of things that we have in common due either to our biology or because of our shared experiences. The main focus of exploration in this chapter is that very difference that was sharply brought home to me by my Charlie Brown error, the differences between the way men and women communicate. The chapter then looks at three more examples of diversity and how it can influence the way we communicate: our personality, our age and our personal experience.

GENDER AND LANGUAGE

Let's look first at men and women. Have you ever been chatting in a mixed group of men and women and noticed that a particular man seems to be dominating the conversation? Or perhaps it is a woman who appears to be interrupting others almost as soon as they begin to speak? You may have asked yourself, 'Is it because he's a man?' or wondered, 'Is she just being bolshie?' In other words, is it all about personality or do women and men really communicate differently? And if men and women do take a different approach to speaking and listening, how is it played out and what are the reasons for these differences?

Here are a number of statements that illustrate some common assumptions about the differences between the way women and men communicate. Which do you agree with? The descriptions and explanations that follow the statements are generalisations only: there is a vast variation within these two gender groups.

» **Women talk more than men.**
» **Men are more likely than women to interrupt other speakers.**
» **Men are the more confident speakers.**
» **Women have more advanced verbal skills.**
» **Women are more likely than men to listen.**

Talking

It is assumed by many of us that women talk more than men and most research supports this although much depends on the context. In the public arena such as meetings and classrooms, men do the most talking. They also have greater success in getting their topics accepted by the group. Yet in the private arena it is women who speak more. Women also begin more conversations and keep conversations going by introducing new topics and by asking questions.

Interrupting

Who is more likely to interrupt you, a man or a woman? This is an easy one. Men are far more likely to interrupt than women. In one study, men interrupted 46 times compared with women only twice. (To find out more Google: Mertz E 'The Language of Law School'.) There is also a difference in the reasons for interrupting. When men interrupt it is more likely to be because they are not paying attention to the speaker. Women, on the other hand, are more likely to interrupt to signal that they are listening, for example by saying 'yes' to indicate agreement.

CONFIDENCE

Men do appear to be the more assertive and authoritative speakers. For example, if a man needs some help he is more likely than a woman to say, 'Could you give me some help?' Women are less likely to impose their ideas and needs on others. When they do, they are more likely to prefix their ideas with, for example, 'It might be a good idea to' in order to soften the impact. If they need help women are more likely to say, 'Do you think you could give me a hand?' Women are also more likely to change a statement into a question by using a rising tone at the end, for example, 'Dinner at seven?' Additionally, they use more tag statements than men. Tag statements are short phrases such as 'isn't it?' or 'shall we?' added on to the end of their statement, for example, 'This chocolate cake is delicious, isn't it?' The point of tag statements is to seek confirmation from another that their opinion is valid.

VERBAL SKILLS

We are often told that women are better than men with words and that they have more advanced verbal skills. Women are, on the whole moderately better at spelling but the assumption that they have better all round verbal skills is not whole-heartedly accepted and some research appears to show little difference between men's and women's verbal skills.

LISTENING

When it comes to listening women do indeed outperform men in this essential skill. They connect more with the emotional and intuitive aspects of a conversation, are more likely to acknowledge what they hear and to encourage others to continue speaking by using words and phrases such as 'Yes' and 'I see'. Men tend to focus on the relevant facts but acknowledge what they have heard less often.

GENDER AND BODY LANGUAGE

If men and women take a different approach to speaking it is only to be expected that they also use different body language: after all, much of our body language is automatic, unconscious and embedded in the evolutionary process. Yet apart from the more obvious gestures such as the male stance with feet planted firmly apart or the female tendency to keep their knees together when sitting, putting your finger on the subtleties of typically male or female body language may not be that straightforward. Nevertheless, just as with language, we do make some assumptions about how men and women differ in the way they engage their bodies when they are speaking.

TRY THIS

Here are a number of statements to illustrate some common assumptions concerning the body language of women and men. Which do you agree with? The descriptions and explanations that follow the statements are generalisations only: there is a vast variation within these two gender groups.

» **Women smile more than men.**
» **Women wave their hands around when they speak.**
» **Men are less skilled at reading body language.**
» **Women make better liars than men.**
» **Men and women use the same signals to attract a partner.**

SMILING

Women do in fact smile far more than men. (To find out more Google: McDuff D 'A large scale analysis of sex differences in facial expressions'.) One theory to account for this difference is that historically, women have taken a more subordinate role and therefore they may use the smile to appease. We know that smiling has an evolutionary role in placation and appeasement and so it could well be the case that a woman might smile to placate and to encourage harmony. Yet appeasement is not the whole story as smiling is also a universal, innate gesture to indicate pleasure. Even at eight weeks old baby girls will smile far more than baby boys so it may well be that women's propensity for smiling more than men is also innate. Women also have more expressive faces than men and a greater range of facial expressions.

HAND GESTURES

Women do use their hands a little more than men when they speak but there isn't a significant difference. Women also stand closer to each other than men stand to other men and are far more likely to touch another woman than a man would be to touch another man.

READING BODY LANGUAGE

Despite some people having a naturally perceptive personality, all the evidence seems to suggest that, on the whole, men are less alert to body language and are not as skilful as women at interpreting it. When shown short films with the sound muted women read the situations accurately 87% time whilst men only 42% of the time. This shouldn't be too surprising as most research reveals that women are more perceptive and intuitive than men, have a greater aptitude for empathy and use it more effectively. (To find out more Google: Pease & Pease 'The Definitive Book of Body Language'.)

TELLING LIES

Women do make better liars than men. Because they are better than men at reading body language and recognising other people's emotions they are also better at manipulating others by lying and when women lie, they also tend to tell more complex lies than men. They have a number of advantages at the start. These advantages appear in the form of instinctive, unconscious gestures that can assist them when they tell a lie. To begin with, women's pupils are able to dilate faster than men's. This enables them to appear more innocent (babies have large pupils) but it also helps them to create a sense of rapport that can camouflage a lie. Women also instinctively mirror (copy) the body language of others more than men; they mirror both men and women and this too will create rapport.

ATTRACTING A PARTNER

Women and men have many body signals to indicate that they feel attraction and a number of them are the same for both sexes such as making eye contact, smiling and turning towards each other. They may also mirror each other's bodies. A good example is if one leans forward or uses a particular gesture such as cupping the chin with the hand, the other may well automatically and unconsciously do the same. In addition to these shared gestures there are some attraction gestures that are specific to men or to women. Men may, for example, take up a power pose, standing tall with elbows slightly out possibly with their hands in their pockets. On the other hand, a gesture used almost exclusively by women is one where they tilt their head to one side and expose the side of the neck. These gender specific gestures are explored in more detail in the following chapter.

WHY MEN AND WOMEN DIFFER

It seems, therefore, that there are some significant differences between men and women regarding the way they use spoken language, the way they engage in conversation and in the way their bodies speak. So what might explain these differences? One possible idea is that evolution has fashioned the behaviour of men and women for different purposes. This theory suggests that historically a man's role has been one more concerned with providing and protecting. Men have traditionally 'brought home the bacon', and ensured that the family group enjoyed safety and security. A woman's role, on the other hand, has throughout time been more of a nurturing role, one that requires well developed verbal skills, a high degree of intuitive perception and adroitness at reading body language.

Women have traditionally taken the major responsibility for caring for and nurturing other members of the group including the child-rearing role. Women who raise children will spend a number of years relying on body language to communicate with young offspring. Their child-rearing experiences, which will have involved paying attention to small details and picking up on even the most subtle of body language signals, will have honed their intuitive skills. This theory finds support in research that shows that men who are engaged in nurturing occupations such as nursing and social work are almost as perceptive and intuitive as women and as skilled in interpreting body language.

Women's greater perceptive and intuitive capabilities have also been explained as an innate, instinctive capacity to pick up on and interpret body language signals. Research using Magnetic Resonance Imaging (MRI) brain scans provides good evidence that this too may well be the case. Comparing the differences in the brains of men and women can also provide us with other clues as to the possible reasons for the differences in communication style between men and women.

The areas in women's brains that are concerned with verbal communication are larger than those in men's brains. When engaged in communicating, the verbal and emotional areas in women's brains show far greater activity than in men. Women's brains also have more hardwiring related to reading other people's emotions than men's brains. This means they have a greater capacity for evaluating other people.

Women are more able to use several areas of their brain to process information. They can send information easily across the different areas of the brain and can also move information from the right creative side of the brain to the left logical side and back again. This can help them to multi-task and also makes it easer for them to work out complex relationships between people. Women's brains are also better organised for juggling a number of unrelated topics at the same time so they can comfortably talk about several unrelated topics in the one conversation. (To find out more Google: Zaidi Z 'Gender Differences in the Human Brain'.)

Whereas women's brains show greater activity in the verbal areas, men's brains show increased activity in the mechanical areas; this gives them a high degree of ability in the spatial arena. In men's brains information also tends to be contained in specific areas of the brain and is more often moved within the same side of the brain. This gives them greater skill in focusing on specifics. Men also tend to have better developed focused vision; this makes them better than women at seeing not only directly in front of them and focusing on a single object but also better equips them for seeing over long distances, all necessary survival skills. (To find out more Google: Zaidi Z 'Gender Differences in Human Brain'.)

It does seem that men's brains have evolved to make them better able to focus on specifics whereas women's brains have evolved to enable them to see the whole picture. The research into the differences between men's and women's brains is not conclusive and it is likely that with increasingly sophisticated technology much more will be revealed to us. Nevertheless, it does seem that the brains of men and women have evolved to accommodate and fulfil different evolutionary demands and we can observe the consequences of those demands played out every time we observe the differences in how men and women communicate.

PERSONALITY

Notwithstanding the demands and limitations of being a man or a woman, the way we communicate with each other is also shaped by our personality and specifically by the degree to which we fall within either the introvert or extrovert bracket. If we lean more towards the introvert the chances are that we will be less interested in engaging in conversation. In a group we will be less keen to contribute and will often be the first to stop speaking, preferring instead to listen and observe. When we do speak we may well use a softer voice and be less animated that others. Our body language may also be distinctive; we may use more closed gestures and body positions, for example we may keep our arms folded or our shoulders slightly hunched and feel less comfortable making eye contact with others.

If, on the other hand, we lean more towards the extrovert we are more likely to begin a conversation with others, talk more, work harder to keep the conversation going and feel more comfortable making eye contact. We are also likely to use more elaborate and open gestures, take up more space and to feel less happy sitting still.

Psychologists tell us that the nervous systems of these two personality types, introvert and extrovert, are different in the way they respond to social interactions. If we are more introverted our nervous system can easily become over stimulated and to avoid this we need time out. On the other hand, if we are more extroverted our nervous system welcomes stimulation and social interaction is immensely enjoyable and satisfying.

AGE

Our age is a significant biological factor that has some bearing on how we communicate. It will shape our choice of words, our manner of speaking and our body language. Younger people, for example, tend to use a vocabulary that older people may see as slang but which is in fact an example of a specific dialect, in this case a youth dialect. Younger people are also far more eager to embrace new and diverse vocabulary. As we age our language tends to become more staid and conventional. When speaking to older generations younger people will tend to talk more slowly and use more pauses.

When it comes to reading the body language of different age groups some are easier to read than others. The easiest people for us to read are those that are closest to us in age. This is simply because we spend most of our time with those of a similar age and so we become familiar with their body language signals.

Of groups in general, children turn out to be the easiest to read. This is because the body signals that children display are clear and unequivocal, for example a child will openly cover his mouth if he makes an error or tells a lie. This clarity makes sense; before they can speak, communicating through body language is the only way for children to ensure their needs are met. As we become older the hand to face gesture is just one example of the many gestures that over time become less obvious. In this case the gesture may become a stroke to the side of the head or a touch to the side of the face with a finger. Our age also influences how often we smile. The best smilers are children who may well smile in excess of 100 times a day. As far as the rest of us are concerned the best of us manage to smile around twenty times a day.

The body language of older people is the hardest to read, especially facial expression. One reason is that older people have less facial muscle tone and so have less exaggerated expressions for us to observe. And if by chance they have had Botox treatment it makes reading their expressions, especially interpreting their emotions almost impossible. Another interesting difference in the body language of older people is that the older they become the more serious they become and this is reflected in the set of their faces.

Experience

Our personal experience is a major influence on the way we communicate. Probably the best example of a personal experience that is particularly relevant to the way we speak is the place where we were born, the place where our roots lie. So, for example, when you go out for afternoon tea and you order from the waiter or waitress, what do you ask for? Do you say that you would like a scone or a scon(e)? And on a cold night when you feel like a good hot soak, will it be in the bath or the ba(h)th?

We are sticklers for our own versions of these words, sometimes engaging in good natured but earnestly fought rivalries with others and prepared to defend to the end our particular idea of the 'proper' word; scone and ba(h)th if you hail from the South of the country and scon(e) and bath if you are from the North. These are just a couple of the numerous examples of a specific way of pronouncing words that we associate with a particular region. The strength of feeling we may experience can be explained by the fact that how we pronounce our words, in other words our accent, is tightly bound up with our identity, with the place we see as our home and the people in that home community that we see as other members of our tribe.

It's not just a matter of pronunciation that marks our affiliation to our roots; our distinctive vocabulary, the words we might use to describe a particular thing, marks us out as local to a particular area. For example, when you go down an alleyway between buildings are you going down a ginnel, a jitty, a jennel, a gully, a snicket or a twitten? Many regional words have enjoyed a long and sound ancestry. Take for example the word 'while'. In some parts of Yorkshire and Lincolnshire, the word 'while' (or whilst) is used rather than the word 'until', so you might hear the phrase, 'Wait while dinner time'. This use of the word 'while' was in place at least as far back as the 14th century and it is probably much older.

TRY THIS

When you sit down to your evening meal would you say that you tuck into your dinner, your tea or your supper and do you then enjoy eating your pudding, your dessert, your sweet or your afters?

The answers you come up with in response to these questions depend on a whole range of factors that may not necessarily be connected to where you were born but are closely linked to your roots. Even when we live in a particular community we might well speak differently, and use different vocabulary from other people in that community and these differences are going to depend to a greater or lesser degree on our family, our education, our career, our lifestyle and our interests.

Our accent (how we pronounce words) our vocabulary (the words we use) and our grammar (how we structure our words into phrases and sentences) are the three elements in the bigger picture that we call dialect. Our dialect is more than an expression of our roots; it is also an expression of our individuality. No two people speak in exactly the same way: personal dialect enables us to recognise others by their voice. Regrettably, when it comes to dialects there is a perceived pecking order. Some dialects are seen as better, more correct or more acceptable than others: Standard (BBC) English is a good example.

This is a sad state of affairs; all speaking is dialect, even those forms of speaking we may be tempted to think of as good models are dialects. The future of regional dialects doesn't look rosy; it is likely that their story will parallel the story of the decline in the numbers and varieties of spoken languages. But in the meantime we need at the very least to embrace, enjoy and celebrate this multiplicity of regional verbal diversity.

WHERE ARE WE NOW?

Gender, age, personality, background and personal experience will each shape the way we communicate with each other.

» Men speak more often in the public arena and are more likely to interrupt other speakers. Women talk more in the private arena and are more likely to listen to others and to encourage others to talk. There are few significant differences between the verbal skills of men and women.

» Women use slightly more hand gestures than men when they speak and they smile more often. They are better at reading body language, recognising emotions and at telling lies. Men and women share some body signals to attract a mate but some signals are specific to men or to women.

» The demands of evolution have shaped men's and women's brains. Women's brains have wider connections making it easier for them to see the bigger picture. The connections in men's brains are more concentrated in certain areas making it easier for them to focus on specifics.

» Our personality can influence our communication style. If we are more introverted our nervous system can easily become over-stimulated by too much social interaction and we need time out. If we are more extroverted we thrive on social interaction.

» Our age has some bearing on both the way we speak and on our body language. Younger people are more likely to use slang; older people's body language is more difficult to interpret.

» Our background, where we were born, our family, our education and our interests will all influence the way we speak.

A strong and recurrent theme that runs throughout this book is the supremacy of our bodies in being able to automatically, instantly and expertly express our emotions. There is a powerful and compelling theory that offers an explanation for why this is the case. This theory is the topic of the final chapter.

12

EVERY BODY FEELS:
HOW BODY LANGUAGE MAY HAVE
HELPED US TO SURVIVE

Why do babies cry when they are born and why is it that a baby's cry is almost impossible to ignore? It's not difficult to work out the reason. Newborns are distressed; their anguished faces and rigid bodies tell their own story. Perhaps it is the distress of being born. On the other hand it may equally be the distress of separation as almost all babies will cry within a few seconds if they are not reunited with their mother. There is a lot at stake for the newborn. Letting the world know that they have been separated from safety and comfort and producing a sound that is hard to ignore will go far to ensuring their survival.

We are really not so different from the newborn. Our bodies will express our emotions for the same reasons, to ensure our survival. A number of our deepest and most powerful emotions stand out to illustrate this: anger, fear, attachment and attraction. This chapter will describe how and why each of these emotions is so easy to observe in our bodies. It will also offer an explanation for why it is that our emotions are evident in every communicative interaction we engage in.

We have different ways of making decisions, different ways of responding to what is happening around us. How we make decisions depends on how quickly we need to respond. For example, if we touch a very hot pan we need to respond extremely rapidly by removing our hand; so fast in fact, that our body makes the decision for us. Our hand shoots away from the pan before we have even realised that we have been burned. This is an ancient response shared by other species and the message (that the pan is hot and is burning us) doesn't even reach our brain before we have removed our hand.

Sometimes we have the luxury of extended time to make our decisions. Take for example, your response if you are asked where you would like to go for a meal. You consider the restaurants you know, the menus, the price and so on, and then you decide. This decision is made in the modern, rational thinking area of our brain. Numerous responses and decisions we make also come from the thinking brain, as does much of our body language, for example, pointing to the chocolate cake in the cake shop, shaking hands when you meet someone and so on.

Yet there are situations where we don't have the luxury of time to make our responses. The decisions we need to make in these situations are not made in the thinking part of the brain because the thinking brain is too slow, it takes too long to respond. Responses that we need to make instantly are sometimes called our 'chimp responses' because we know that they are made in the ancient primitive part of the brain. So when do we need to make instant decisions?

It is difficult for us to imagine ourselves in the place of our distant ancestors, before farming, before settled communities and the security provided by a permanent home and belonging to a sizeable group. We know that for long periods in our human evolution we could have faced danger on a daily basis. We may have faced potentially hostile humans or dangerous animals and would have needed to decide very quickly on the best way to deal with them. To be of any use to us these decisions would need to be made instantly; our very life might have depended on their outcome. There would be no time to stop and think or to consult a focus group. The hostile human or the wild animal would have made minced meat of us whilst we were making up our minds.

In this precarious situation we would have had a limited number of options. One option would be to attack whatever was threatening us and the other, to run away from it as fast as possible. For these two options two powerful emotions, anger and fear, are at play. They are better known as our fight/flight responses and they have a significant and observable effect on our bodies. The first thing that would happen, and it would happen instantly, would be an increase in both our breathing rate and our heart rate. These changes would allow us to take more oxygen into our lungs and to send this oxygen to our body muscles. This would increase our energy level for what lies ahead, to fight or to run. So how would these changes be observed in our bodies?

Let's say that anger is the dominant emotion that is driving our response and we are prepared to face the threat. For this option we would need to signal that we were ready and prepared for the fight. We would need to make our intentions visible. Our muscles would be tensed, our bodies drawn up to full height, legs planted firmly apart to give us the balance necessary to fight. Our fists would be clenched ready to throw the first punch. Our faces would take on an aggressive expression, eyes focused sharply and glaringly on the threat to ensure that it knew we had it in our sights. Our lips would be pulled back, mouth open to show our teeth, ready to take the first bite. Pulling our lips back in this way with our mouths open flattens our noses and widens our nostrils; with wider nostrils we can take more air into our body.

TRY THIS

> Stand in front of a mirror and make an aggressive face. Pull your lips back with your mouth open as if you are about to bite. You will be able feel more air going into your nostrils as they widen. It is best to do this when you are alone because it isn't a pretty expression!

That great observer, William Shakespeare described this very expression in that famous 'Once more into the breach…' speech, when King Henry is giving his troops a pep talk before the battle. Henry says, 'Now lend the eye a terrible aspect, now set the teeth and stretch the nostrils wide'. In this speech Henry is instructing his men go out and scare the pants off the enemy.

Sometimes it's not anger but fear that is the dominant emotion driving our response and we have one thing on our mind, to make a quick exit. Our bodies would respond in the same way as they do when we are angry; that same increase in our breathing rate and heart rate. This time our heart is pumping oxygenated blood around our body, to provide us with energy, not to fight, but to run.

TRY THIS

> Think back to an occasion when you were feeling anxious or frightened. Perhaps you were in the dentist's waiting room and were about to have a tooth extracted. Can you recall how your body responded to your fear?

You may have been aware of your heart pumping. You may have remembered feeling hot or shaky or both. This is because your body was preparing to run away by providing you with extra energy but the situation didn't allow you to make use of this extra energy in any physical way.

There is a third option we could on call on when faced with threat: we could

attempt to appease whatever is threatening us. For the appeasement option to work we would need to signal that we were of no importance, that we were meek and submissive, throwing ourselves on the mercy of whatever is threatening us. We have an excellent appeasement expression, the smile. Chimpanzees have been observed smiling to appease. We might also try to make ourselves look smaller, and therefore harmless by looking down or away or even bending a little. A number of other species bend low to appease.

You may well be wondering at this point how relevant these options are for us today. We are after all, sophisticated humans living in a modern world. There is a noticeable lack of dangerous animals roaming our streets and, on the whole, most humans we meet are friendly rather than hostile. Yet we still have numerous threats.

Granted they are not usually life threatening, but threats nonetheless and our bodies still respond to them in the way they know best. In doing so they signal our age-old emotions of anger and fear. So what do our bodies do? To answer that question think what your immediate gut response might be if someone tried to grab your handbag or the wallet out of your pocket. You've got it: you hang on to your handbag or wallet like grim death even though rational thinking would tell you this is not a good idea.

Now consider another scenario: it is one that isn't dangerous yet it is one that can still trigger our fight response. You are late for an appointment as you drive your car into a very full car park. You look around for a space to park. You drive around for a few minutes hoping that someone will soon leave. Finally you spot what you are looking for. Over on the far side of the car park, a car is pulling out. You make your way towards it, dutifully following the one-way arrows, but just as you almost reach it a car enters the car park through the exit and drives straight into your parking space.

What do you do? Rational thinking would tell you to shrug your shoulders and look for another parking place but remember, rational thinking is a little slow in getting off the ground. Your immediate response is likely to show in your face: annoyance, irritation, frustration and anger, your forehead deeply furrowed, your eyes glaring and your mouth grim. These visible responses are to signal that you are ready for the fight. Your shoulders might well be hunched and your hands fisted ready to make the first punch. Would your lips be drawn back to show your teeth, ready to take the first bite? Perhaps, if you are feeling angry enough, but on the whole, we sophisticated modern humans seldom bite. The problem is our bodies haven't quite yet learned this so they respond in the way they know well. Your closed lips might well draw back into what we call the 'tight mouth'.

This situation makes us feel angry because we have just faced a threat and generally, when we feel angry there is some perceived threat at the heart of our anger, although it isn't always easy to identify what that threat actually is. The threat in this example is in the form of a thief, a thief who has stolen something that rightly belongs to us, our car parking space. A willingness and preparedness to fight off a perceived threat and to signal our intention to do so is vital to ensure our survival.

Now take a situation where we may feel more frightened than angry. Let's say it is the middle the night; you are alone and are suddenly woken up by a crash of glass and you then hear voices from downstairs. There is no ambiguity about the threat here; you are afraid you are about to be murdered in your bed. How might your body respond to this threat? What would it wish to do? Well it is unlikely to want to face the threat; it might just freeze and hope that it won't be noticed but perhaps a better option would be to run.

Luckily this threat is rare but we still have threats that cause our bodies to respond in the same way. Here are two examples. You are about to give a talk to a group of people. You are feeling nervous about facing your audience. Or you are on your way to an important job interview and you are held up in an unexpected traffic jam. You know you are going to arrive late and are feeling anxious.

Let us first deal with the perceived threat. What exactly is the threat in these two examples? In the first it is most likely to be the threat of embarrassment if, when you begin to speak, you forget your words, you clam up and everyone stares at you. In the second example the threat is similar but is perhaps more akin to shame because others will view you as incompetent and tardy with your time keeping. There is also the threat of a poor outcome for your job interview.

We experience fear differently and we don't all feel frightened by the same things. Despite this our responses are pretty much identical, regardless of what is causing our fear. So what do our bodies do? Remember, when we are feeling frightened what we really want to do is to run away. Unsurprisingly this option for we modern humans is rarely available. There is little doubt that we'd feel very silly when about to give a talk if we made a quick dive for the door. So if running away is not available to us, another option is to hide. Again, this is rarely possible; we would look even sillier crouching down and hiding behind our chair.

We seem to have no choices left. We know that we cannot run or hide. Yet what do our bodies know? They still believe we can. When we are frightened our bodies take that first step to running away; we back off. We might avert our eyes from the perceived threat and either move back or lean our bodies away. So, for example, in a room full of strangers, if we are feeling anxious and tense, our bodies ensure that we retain space for that quick getaway.

Our bodies also believe that we can hide. Not only do they believe this but they also provide us with something to hide behind, a barrier that is not too noticeable to ensure that we don't look silly. This barrier is provided by our hands and arms. When we are feeling anxious, frightened or nervous we unconsciously move our hands and arms to the front our body. If we are standing, we may clasp our hands together or place one hand either low down against the other arm or high, almost at shoulder height. We may cross our arms over the front of our body as in a self-hug. If we are holding something, say a handbag or a file, we may bring it to the front of our body. If we are sitting down we may clasp our hands on our laps or cross our arms. Each of these gestures is designed to act as a barrier, to protect us from the perceived threat and offer us some comfort.

We are fortunate indeed that we possess these two powerful emotions, anger and fear that have driven our responses to perceived threats and so helped to ensure our survival. Yet our flight/fight responses did not and indeed, do not operate in isolation. Our chances of survival increased from the advantages gained from two further emotions that we possess, attachment and attraction.

ATTACHMENT

Consider the following scenario. You are in a group of people and one person begins to yawn. What can sometimes happen next? Yes, before long some of you will begin to yawn. Here is another example. You are with a group of friends, one of you says something very funny and you all begin to laugh. The more you laugh the more you realise you are laughing simply because everyone is laughing. Both yawning and laughing are highly contagious as are many other gestures we make.

Here is another scenario. Someone slams a car door and accidentally shuts their finger in the door. How does your body react? The chances are that it will flinch – a gut wrench. This will be an instant response, before you have even registered what has happened. You may even have felt a slight gut wrench as you read these words. Why is this the case?

What our bodies are doing when we 'catch' a yawn or a laugh from someone or respond to another's pain is mimicking or mirroring another human body, an emotional connection we can feel to other members of our human group. I have called this connection 'attachment': you may also think of it as empathy or fellow feeling.

Whichever label you choose to describe it, attachment is a powerful, instinctive and automatic response catalysed by a network of only recently discovered mirror neurons. (To find out more Google: Rizzolattie & Gallses, University of Palma.) These neurons are activated when we observe someone perform an activity in the same way as they would be activated if we were to perform it ourselves. One possible explanation for the origins of mirror neurons may be in allowing us to learn skills by observing another person, for example tool making.

Yet there is another even more compelling explanation that may lie in our evolution. These mirror neurons may have been instrumental in enabling us to signal our attachment to other members of our human group. To explain why we have this ability we need to return yet again to that early period in our evolutionary history when our primitive ancestors lived in small groups. It is fair to say that during this long period in our history, belonging to a group was a matter of life or death. It is extremely unlikely that we would have survived isolated from our group. Even now we modern humans don't flourish in isolation. In truth, we know that loneliness is so bad for us it can even lead to an early death.

Our ability to mirror our fellow humans may well have been a way to ensure our attachment to our group and so gain the protection that group membership offers. Mirroring is a more interesting gesture than first appearances might suggest. Let us say you have met up with a friend, or that a member of your family comes to talk with you and you see immediately from their face that they are upset about something. Now before they even begin to tell you their problem your body will respond to the distress in their face. As you observe their expression, the muscles of your face will contract just a little. Your mouth might turn down slightly, perhaps a slight frown will begin to appear on your brow as your body attempts to mirror theirs. You are unlikely to be aware that this is happening.
Even more interesting is what happens next. The muscles in your face that have contracted will then send a message to your brain to instruct it to take on a feeling of distress. It will try to take on the feelings experienced by your friend or family member. This ability we have to mirror and so share, not only other people's body

language but their feelings, has been described by the Dutch zoologist Franz De Waal. His research leads him to believe that here, within the physical, biological sphere, lies the true origin of empathy. It appears to be an innate ability, one that is shared by many animal species. (To find out more Google: De Waal F 'The Age of Empathy'.)

We are born knowing how to mirror. Within minutes of birth a newborn is able to mimic the expressions on the face of the adult who is holding it. If the adult pokes out her tongue or opens her mouth wide, within a few seconds the newborn may well do the same. Within a few months babies are able to mirror not only the expressions but the emotions they observe in those around them and will often cry if they see a parent or older sibling crying.

We mirror within families, especially when the family members are close. Observe couples when you are next dining out in a restaurant. You can often see them using the same arm or body gestures: this could be hands folded in laps, an elbow on the table or both sitting forward in their seats and so on. We mirror those with whom we have an affinity, a shared identity or shared history: old friends, long-standing members of particular social group and so on.

We may even mirror in order to co-operate. Those engaged in tricky negotiations will sometimes unconsciously mirror each other. Sometimes you will see the bodies of politicians who you know don't get on with each other mirror each other in spite of their less than positive relationship. It is almost as if their bodies are searching for a way forward in the negotiations but have omitted to let their owners in on the plan.

As a general rule we mirror in small groups and seldom in large groups but there are a few exceptions. We mirror in a large group if the group has a very strong group identity. One example of this strong identity is sport and football in particular. Football supporters belong to a large but close-knit group with a strong shared group identity.

TRY THIS

If you enjoy watching football matches, the next time you watch, keep your eyes open for mirroring. A good example is when a player

152

stupidly misses a goal or pass that they, and everyone else knows that they should have got. The player's hands may well go straight to cover their eyes, 'I can't believe I didn't see that', or to cradle their head, 'I don't understand why I missed that'. If this happens, there is a good chance that fellow team members and possibly numerous fans will instinctively and immediately follow suit. They wouldn't have thought about doing so nor will they know in advance or even as it happens what their bodies are doing.

It has been suggested by the British zoologist, Desmond Morris, that our ability to mirror each other may well have its roots way back in our evolutionary history. It could well originate in that ability shared by many animal species, especially birds and herd animals, to instantly and instinctively mirror each other in order to avoid a threat. And it seems that we have not quite lost this ability and it performs the same function for us as it does for animal species, to increase our chances of survival. (To find out more Google: Morris D 'Manwatching'.)

ATTRACTION

The final emotion that is so closely connected to our survival is attraction. Having ensured our attachment to our group or tribe we can think about attracting a mate. Now you might ask yourself 'What has finding a mate got to do with survival?' Quite a lot in fact, but this is not about survival of the individual but the survival of our species. Without mating, few species can produce offspring; without offspring no species can survive.

The previous chapter described the variety of body signals used by men and women to attract a partner. Two of these signals, the head tilt used by women and the power gesture used by men are worth a closer look. A woman may tilt her head to one side to attract a male, a gesture that causes her neck to be exposed. This gesture was first identified and recorded as a sign of sexual attraction by Charles Darwin. (To find out more Google: Darwin C 'The Expression of the Emotions in Man and Animals'.)

Since Darwin's time the head tilt has been well exploited commercially. Numerous images have been created by artists, film-makers and advertisers showing women using this signal. On the other hand it is a gesture rarely seen in images of men. The roots of this gesture may lie in appeasement. A weaker animal will sometimes use the head tilt to appease a more dominant animal. The head tilt exposes the neck and therefore offers access to the jugular vein. The message in this gesture, when used by animals is pretty much, 'I am weak. You can go for the kill (the jugular vein) if you so choose'. Normally in this situation the dominant animal will recognise this message and back off, satisfied that its position and status have not been compromised.

When used by women this gesture is thought to carry a similar meaning. Here it is a sign of attraction because it portrays the woman as vulnerable and in need of protection. You may think this signal means that she needs protection for herself but this is not the case. It is thought that the protection she needs is for her potential offspring. This signal may well appeal to the male characteristic to protect and cherish weaker individuals. In evolutionary terms this makes perfect sense because it provides a way for women to ensure protection for her future offspring and thus increase the chances of survival the species.

One male gesture that indicates that they feel attracted is to put their hands to their hips, often with thumbs in pockets and fingers pointing downward. This gesture conveys the message that the man is strong, sufficiently strong to protect potential offspring. Again, in evolutionary terms this gesture also makes sense. As far as the fingers pointing down are concerned, you can probably make up your own mind! These attraction gestures used by men and women help to ensure the survival of our human species.

Where are we now?

The evolutionary roots of many of our emotional responses, expressed through our bodies, may lie in ensuring our survival.

- » When faced with a threat we express anger and fear through our bodies.
- » We are able to mirror the bodies of others in our group or tribe especially those we are close to in order to establish our place within it and gain the protection it offers.
- » We signal attraction in order to ensure the survival of our species.

AFTERWORD

In these pages you have read about how and why we use our voices, our facial expressions, gestures and our whole body to communicate with each other. You have participated in the lighter side of English and relished our skill at manipulating it. You have learned what some experts have to say about how and why we learned to speak and about how language develops and evolves. Lastly, you have delved into the intricacies and complexities of the way we communicate with each and discovered how clever we are at getting our messages across sometimes despite all the odds.

The remarkable story of what we humans have achieved is bound up with our exceptional skills at communicating. Every time we engage in dialogue with another person we transform an activity that can only be described as immensely complex into one that we make look simple. We use language with ease, manipulating it at will for our advantage and enjoyment. Our desire to co-operate and collaborate with each other has ensured our outstanding success.

This story of our success is equalled only by that told of our ability to communicate effortlessly with each other through the language of our bodies. It is a story of our desire to connect with each other and to share our thoughts and especially our emotions. It is the story of our survival first told by Charles Darwin and is a celebration of our phenomenal expertise.

I do hope that you have enjoyed this book. If you would like to keep in touch please email me at nancy.appleyard@hotmail.com

Matador

For exclusive discounts on Matador titles,
sign up to our occasional newsletter at
troubador.co.uk/bookshop